Essential
Barcelona

by Teresa Fisher

Above: *Spanish blue skies over the fountain of Parc de la Ciutadella*

PASSPORT BOOKS
NTC/Contemporary Publishing Group

Above: *Barcelona has a strong musical tradition*

Front cover: *Flamenco dancer; Parc Güell gatehouse; Gaudian detail*
Back cover: *seafood paella*

First published in 1999 by Passport Books, a division of NTC/Contemporary Publishing Group, Inc.
4255 West Touhy Avenue, Lincolnwood (Chicago), Illinois 60712-1975, U.S.A.

Copyright © The Automobile Association 1998
Maps © The Automobile Association 1998

The Automobile Association retains the copyright in the original edition © 1998 and in all subsequent editions, reprints, and amendments.

All rights reserved. No part of this book may be reproduced, stored in a retrieval system, or transmitted in any form or by any means, electronic, mechanical, photocopying, recording, or otherwise, without the prior permission of NTC/Contemporary Publishing Group, Inc.

The contents of this publication are believed correct at the time of printing. Nevertheless, the publishers cannot accept responsibility for errors or omissions, or for changes in details given. We are always grateful to readers who let us know of any errors or omissions they come across, and future printings will be updated accordingly.

Published by Passport Books in conjunction with The Automobile Association of Great Britain.

Written by Teresa Fisher

Library of Congress Catalog Card Number: 99-74042
ISBN 0-8442-2212-7

Color separation: Pace Colour, Southampton

Printed and bound in Italy by Printer Trento srl

Contents

About this Book 4

Viewing Barcelona 5–14
- Teresa Fisher's Barcelona   6
- Barcelona's Features   7
- Essence of Barcelona   8–9
- The Shaping of Barcelona   10–11
- Peace and Quiet   12–13
- Barcelona's Famous   14

Top Ten 15–26
- Catedral   16
- Fundació Joan Miró   17
- Montjuïc   18
- Museu Nacional d'Art de Catalunya   19
- Museu Picasso   20
- Parc Güell   21
- Poble Espanyol   22
- La Rambla   23
- La Sagrada Família   24–5
- Santa Maria del Mar   26

What to See 27–90
- Barcelona   28–77
- Food and Drink   52–3
- In the Know   74–5
- Exploring Catalonia   78–90

Where To... 91–116
- Eat and Drink   92–100
- Stay   101–3
- Shop   104–9
- Take the Children   110–11
- Be Entertained   112–16

Practical Matters 117–24

Index 125–6

Acknowledgements 126

About this Book

KEY TO SYMBOLS

- 🛉 map reference to the maps in the What to See section
- ✉ address
- ☎ telephone number
- 🕓 opening times
- 🍴 restaurant or café on premises or near by
- 🚇 nearest underground train station
- 🚌 nearest bus/tram route
- 🚆 nearest overground train station
- 🚢 nearest ferry stop
- ♿ facilities for visitors with disabilities
- ✋ admission charge
- ↔ other places of interest near by
- ❓ other practical information
- ▶ indicates the page where you will find a fuller description

Essential *Barcelona* is divided into five sections to cover the most important aspects of your visit to Barcelona.

Viewing Barcelona pages 5–14
An introduction to Barcelona by the author.
  Barcelona's Features
  Essence of Barcelona
  The Shaping of Barcelona
  Peace and Quiet
  Barcelona's Famous

Top Ten pages 15–26
The author's choice of the Top Ten places to see in Barcelona, listed in alphabetical order, each with practical information.

What to See pages 27–90
The two main areas of Barcelona, each with its own brief introduction and an alphabetical listing of the main attractions.
  Practical information
  Snippets of 'Did you know…' information
  6 suggested walks
  2 suggested drives
  2 features

Where To... pages 91–116
Detailed listings of the best places to eat, stay, shop, take the children and be entertained.

Practical Matters pages 117–24
A highly visual section containing essential travel information.

Maps
All map references are to the individual maps found in the What to See section of this guide.

For example, Tibidabo has the reference 🛉 47D5 – indicating the page on which the map is located and the grid square in which the hill is to be found. A list of the maps that have been used in this travel guide can be found in the index.

Prices
Where appropriate, an indication of the cost of an establishment is given by **£** signs:

£££ denotes higher prices, **££** denotes average prices, while **£** denotes lower charges.

Star Ratings
Most of the places described in this book have been given a separate rating:

✪✪✪   Do not miss
✪✪   Highly recommended
✪   Worth seeing

Viewing Barcelona

Teresa Fisher's Barcelona	6
Barcelona's Features	7
Essence of Barcelona	8–9
The Shaping of Barcelona	10–11
Peace and Quiet	12–13
Barcelona's Famous	14

Above: *Gaudí chimney faces – the 'witch-scarers' – at Casa Milá*
Right: *a proud Catalan*

VIEWING BARCELONA

Teresa Fisher's Barcelona

Orienting Yourself
Downtown Barcelona is divided into distinctive districts including *La Ribera*, today a popular museum quarter; *El Raval* (or *Barri Xinés*, China Town), a run-down area with a high crime rate (and perhaps best avoided); the bohemian 'village' of *Grácia*; *Barceloneta*, the former fishermen's quarter; and smart seafront developments – *Port Vell*, the Olympic village and port.

Below: *Christopher Columbus surveys the port*
Below right: *aerial view of Passeig de Grácia – one of Barcelona's main thoroughfares*

Inventive and innovative, radical and racy, Barcelona is one of Europe's most dynamic cities. Strolling through its streets is like wandering through a living museum, a legacy of its remarkable two thousand years of history. From the ancient maze-like Gothic quarter, built within the Roman city walls, to the astonishing regimental grid plan of the turn-of-the-century Eixample district, studded with eye-catching jewels of *Modernista* architecture, and the space-age constructions for the 1992 Olympiad, the city contains some of the finest and most eccentric art and architecture in the world. Outstanding even by Barcelonan standards is Gaudí's extraordinary Sagrada Família – for many, reason enough to visit the city.

Just as *Modernisme* – the movement that has made Barcelona unique – emerged at the end of the 19th century as a desire for change and renovation, so today the city is celebrating its past. Rather than suffer a post-Olympic slump, it is restoring its old buildings, introducing new art and architecture and eradicating some severe urban problems, while staying at the forefront of contemporary culture.

As a result, Barcelona today is very much alive – a city bursting with new pride and self-confidence, which cannot fail to excite and delight. So before you leave, consider the city's motto – *Barcelona Es Teva* ('Barcelona Belongs to You') – and drink from the famous Canaletes fountain on La Rambla. It is said that after just one sip, you will fall under the city's spell and are sure to return again, and again... and again.

VIEWING BARCELONA

Barcelona's Features

Geography
- Barcelona is in northeastern Spain, 160km from the French border. The city occupies 99sq km, with 13km of Mediterranean coastline, including 5km of sandy beaches. It is bounded by the mountains of Montjuïc (to the south) and Tibidabo (to the northwest), and framed by the rivers Llobregat (to the south) and Besós (to the north).

Climate
- Barcelona enjoys a Mediterranean climate. Summers are hot and humid with an average temperature of 24°C. Winters are mild and sunny with an average temperature of 11°C. December can be very wet.

People and Economy
- Barcelona's population is 1,707, 286 (or 4,228,048 within the *area metropolitana* of greater Barcelona). Many inhabitants originated from southern Spain, drawn to Catalonia in the 1950s and 60s by the prospect of work in the capital of Spain's most progressive and most prosperous region.

Leisure Facilities
- Barcelona boasts 50 museums and galleries, 123 cinemas, 40 theatres, 2 amusement parks, 2 luxury marinas, a zoo, 6 beaches, 53 parks and gardens and over 2,300 restaurants. A special tourist bus (*bus turístic*) connects 18 of the most popular attractions. Thanks to the 1992 Olympics, the city has top facilities for every kind of sport.

Catalunya (Catalonia)
The autonomous region of Catalunya (Catalonia) covers an area of 31,930sq km (6.3 per cent of Spain) and has a population of over 6 million (15 per cent of the Spanish population), 70 per cent of whom live in greater Barcelona. It is Spain's leading economic region, producing 20 per cent of the country's gross national production. Nearly 40 per cent of all visitors to Spain come to Catalonia.

Above: *children play in the famous Canaletes fountain on La Rambla*

VIEWING BARCELONA

Essence of Barcelona

Below: *Plaça d'Espanya*
Bottom: *aerial view of the city from the Columbus monument*

Barcelona is unique. It has something for everyone and is one of Europe's top destinations. The only problem you will encounter is that there will never be enough time to explore its many museums and monuments, churches and galleries, its fascinating seaboard and, above all, its delectable cuisine.

To enjoy your stay to the full, you will need to adopt the Barcelonan lifestyle – a striking blend of businesslike efficiency combined with long alfresco lunches, lazy siestas, ritual evening *passeixus* (promenades) and an intoxicating nightlife. You will long remember its proud yet generous people, who will welcome you back with open arms when you return, as you surely will.

VIEWING BARCELONA

THE 10 ESSENTIALS

If you have only a short time to visit Barcelona and would like to get a really complete picture of the city, here are the essentials:

- **Stroll along La Rambla** (➤ 23), pause for a coffee and listen to the street performers.
- **Get into Gaudí**, especially Casa Milà (➤ 37), Parc Güell (➤ 21), and the famous Sagrada Família (➤ 24–5).
- **Follow in the footsteps** of Picasso and Dalí and wander at length through the maze of narrow streets in the Barri Gòtic (➤ 40–1).
- **Enjoy the wide variety** of *tapas* (➤ 91–9) available in the local bars.
- **Join locals to dance** the *sardana*, the national dance of Catalonia (➤ 69).
- **Experience the tastes**, fragrances and colours of the Mediterranean at Mercat de la Boqueria (➤ 49).
- **Visit Museu Picasso** (➤ 20).
- **Shop for Spanish fashion** and designer gifts in the smart Eixample district (➤ 42–3).
- **Watch FC Barça play** a home match (➤ 54–5).
- **Walk the waterfront** (➤ 71) and sample the freshest of seafood.

Below: *the entrance to Parc Güell*
Bottom: *human tower building in the city's Castellets festival*

The Shaping of Barcelona

c15 BC
Roman colony of Barcino founded. Roman stone city walls built in AD 4.

531
Barcelona becomes a Visigothic capital.

711
Arabs gain control of Barcelona and call it Barjelunah.

801
Barcelona seized by Franks, making it part of Charlemagne's empire.

878
Guifré el Pilós (Wilfred 'The Hairy') founds the independent county of Catalonia.

1131–62
Reign of Count Ramon Berenguer IV of Barcelona and union of Catalonia and Aragon. Barcelona becomes a major trading city.

1213–76
Reign of Jaume I.

1229
Jaume I conquers Mallorca, then Ibiza (1235), then Valencia (1238) from the Moors.

1249
Council of One Hundred (*Consell de Cent*) set up as the municipal government of Barcelona.

1298
Gothic Cathedral begun.

1323–4
Conquest of Corsica and Sardinia demonstrates Barcelona's maritime supremacy.

1354
The *Corts Catalans*, legislative council of Catalonia, establishes the *Generalitat* to control city finances.

1355
Thousands of Jews massacred in Barcelona's *Call*.

1356
Martí I, last ruler of the House of Barcelona, dies heirless. Catalonia ruled ineffectively from Madrid.

1462-73
Catalan civil war and deterioration of the economy.

1492
Final expulsion of Jews. Discovery of America.

1516
Charles of Habsburg (Charles V), King of Spain.

Bloody history – leaders of the Setmana Tràgica rising are executed

1640
Catalan *Guerra dels Segadors* (Revolt of the Reapers) against Castilian rule.

1714
City falls to Franco-Spanish army during the War of the Spanish Succession. The *Nova Planta* (1715) decree abolishes Catalan institutions and Catalonia becomes a mere province of Spain.

1775
Paving of La Rambla begins.

VIEWING BARCELONA

1808–13
Departure of Napoleonic troops following five years of French occupation.

1832
Spain's first steam-driven factory opens in Barcelona.

1844
Liceu opera house first opened.

1859
Cerdà's plan for the Eixample is approved.

1882
Work begins on the Sagrada Família.

1888
Universal Exhibition attracts 2 million visitors.

Late 19th to early 20th century
The Eixample district is created, containing many *Modernista* buildings.

1899
FC Barcelona founded. First electric trams.

1909
Churches and convents looted and burned by anti-establishment rioters during *Setmana Tràgica* (Tragic Week).

1914–18
Spanish neutrality in World War I helps boost Barcelona's economy.

1921
First metro line opened.

1929
International Exhibition on Montjuïc.

1931
Second Spanish Republic. Francesc Macià declares Catalan independence.

1936
Franco comes to power but his army uprising is defeated by armed city workers. Civil War begins.

1939
City falls to Nationalists. Franco's troops occupy Catalonia. Catalan language is banned and Catalan culture is crushed during subsequent dictatorship. Economic decline.

1975
Following Franco's death, Juan Carlos I is declared king, and acknowledges the re-establishment of the *Generalitat* as the Parliament of an autonomous regional government of Catalonia.

1992
Barcelona Olympic Games on Montjuïc.

1993
Liceu opera house gutted by fire (scheduled to re-open in 2001).

1995–6
The opening of three new museums – the Museu Nacional d'Art de Catalonia, the Museu d'Història de Catalonia and the Museu d'Art Contemporani de Barcelona – reflects continuing pride in the Catalan nation.

2004
Barcelona will host the Universal Forum of Cultures, sponsored by UNESCO.

The 1992 Olympics helped put Barcelona back on the world map

VIEWING BARCELONA

Peace & Quiet

Take a rest from sightseeing and visit one of the city's many beautiful parks

Parc de la Ciutadella in the centre of Barcelona

Barcelona is not a quiet city, yet it is always possible to find small pockets of peace – a quiet alley, a hidden square, a fountain-filled park – and the expansive greenery of Barcelona's twin mountains, Montjuïc (➤ 18) and Tibidabo (➤ 73), provides a joyful respite from frenetic city life. Alternatively, leave behind the hustle and bustle of Barcelona, and head instead for the Catalan countryside, where you will find a naturalist's paradise, blessed with more than its fair share of magnificent scenery, flora and fauna.

The Coast

Although many of the beaches in Barcelona's immediate vicinity have been spoilt, further afield lies some of the Mediterranean's most attractive coastal scenery. To the north, the charming maritime towns and villages, the warm turquoise sea, craggy cliffs and spacious sandy beaches have made the Costa Brava (wild coast) one of the most famous coastlines in Spain. Despite mass tourism, it is still possible to find small, welcoming and surprisingly unspoilt coves, their steep banks cloaked in wild flowers and cactus plants.

To the south of Barcelona, beyond the long, wide, sandy beaches of the Costa Daurada (golden coast, ➤ 87), running from Alcanar and Vilanova i la Geltrú, is the vast Ebro Delta – the second largest wetland habitat on the Mediterranean and home to over 300 species of bird. The area has been made a protected nature reserve, due to the importance of its wildlife and its diversity of habitats – ranging from rice paddies to sand dunes maintained by marram grass, and from riverside woods of white poplar and water-willow to freshwater lagoons framed by reeds and rushes. Look out for otters, white-toothed shrews and water voles, flamingos, purple herons, spadefoot toads, stripeless tree frogs and spiny-footed lizards.

The Hinterland

Catalonia's hinterland offers a variety of landscapes. Just inland from the coast, the hills are clad in Aleppo pines, stone pines and cork oaks, and splashed with the yellows and mauves of broom, gorse, heathers and orchids. Further inland, one of Catalonia's

special delights is to ramble through the region's extensive, sun-baked scrubland habitats of olives, kermes oaks and strawberry trees. The air is fragrant with lavender and wild herbs, their sweet, heady perfume attracting a busy insect life of butterflies, bugs and beetles – an endless feast for the local hoopoes, bee-eaters and warblers. Southwest of Barcelona in the Alt Penedès wine region (► 84–5), where the land is striped with a patchwork of tidy vines, the dramatic gorges of the Serra d'Ancosa, beyond, shelter wild boar and genets, salamanders, badgers, goshawks, tawny owls and other birds of prey.

Above: *a complete change of scene – the impressive mountains of Ordesa National Park*
Below: *getting away from it all: Cardona in the foothills of the Pyrenees*

The Mountains

If you have a couple of days to spare, a trip to the craggy, snow-topped Pyrenees provides a complete contrast to the Mediterranean coast surrounding Barcelona. The Aigüestortes, Estany de Sant Maurici and Ordesa National Parks provide sanctuary for chamois, wild boar and other mountain species. Glacial lagoons, jagged granite formations and verdant valleys with myriad alpine flowers and forests of sober black pine represent the quintessence of this great mountain range. One of the most important preserves of upland wildlife in Europe, the Pyrenean range is every walker's dream.

VIEWING BARCELONA

Barcelona's Famous

Arantxa Sanchez Vicario
One of the greatest tennis players Spain has ever produced, Arantxa was born in Barcelona in 1971. She has won over 75 major titles including the French Open in 1989. Between tournaments she returns home to her family and joins the rest of Barcelona, shopping on the Diagonal, walking her dogs in the Collserola mountains and socialising at Port Vell or Port Olimpic.

Wilfred 'The Hairy'
Few people have heard of Count Guifré 'el Pilós' (c860–98), yet not only was he the first to unite several northeastern counties, creating the basis for a future Catalan state, but he also declared Barcelona capital of the region and founded the dynasty of the Counts of Barcelona. Sadly he met an early death, in battle against the Saracens. It is said that, in recognition of his heroism, the Emperor dipped his fingers into Wilfred's bloody wounds then ran them down his golden shield, thereby creating the four red stripes of today's Catalan flag – the *Quatre Barres* (Four Bars), the oldest flag in Europe.

Antoni Gaudí
Gaudí (1852–1926), Barcelona's most famous son, occupies a unique position in the history of modern architecture. He was a true genius of the *Modernista* movement, without predecessor or successor. To this day his flamboyant art is unique. For many people, Gaudí alone is sufficient reason to visit Barcelona, to see his remarkable organic structures, his trademark pinnacles, towers and rooftop terraces and, above all, the Church of the Sagrada Família (➤ 24–5).Tragically, Gaudí was run over by a tram on the Gran Via and died unrecognised in hospital. When his identity was discovered, Barcelona gave him what was almost a state funeral.

Pablo Ruiz Picasso
Málaga-born Picasso (1881–1973) spent many of his formative years (from the age of 14 to 23) in Barcelona, and is said to have considered himself more Catalan than Andalucian. He was particularly fond of the Catalan capital and, even after his move to Paris in 1904, continued to visit Barcelona regularly, until the Civil War (the subject of his famous painting, *Guernica*) put an end to his visits. Museu Picasso (➤ 20), the city's most visited museum, is particularly rich in paintings from his Barcelona period.

Left: *Picasso never forgot his early adulthood spent in Barcelona*
Above left: *Arantxa Sanchez Vicario*

Top Ten

Catedral	16
Fundació Joan Miró	17
Montjuïc	18
Museu Nacional d'Art de Catalunya	19
Museu Picasso	20
Parc Güell	21
Poble Espanyol	22
La Rambla	23
La Sagrada Família	24–5
Santa Maria del Mar	26

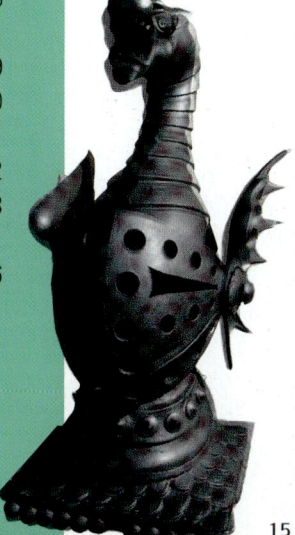

Above: *Casa Bruno Quadras on La Rambla*
Right: *Gaudí ironwork*

TOP TEN

1
Catedral

✢ 62C3

✉ Plaça de la Seu

☎ 93 315 15 54

🕐 Daily 8–1:30, 4–7:30

Ⓜ Jaume I

🚌 17, 19, 40, 45

♿ Few

✋ Free;

↔ Ciutat Vella (➤ 38–9); Museu Frederic Marès (➤ 55); Museu d'Història de la Ciutat (➤ 56); Plaça del Rei (➤ 68)

Museum

☎ 93 310 25 80

🕐 Daily 11–1

✋ Cheap

Barcelona's great cathedral is not only one of the most celebrated examples of Catalan Gothic style, but also one of the finest cathedrals in Spain.

The cathedral is located at the heart of the Barri Gòtic (➤ 40), on the remains of an early Christian basilica and a Romanesque church. Most of the building was erected between the late 13th century and the middle of the 15th century, although the heavily ornate main façade and octagonal dome were constructed at the beginning of the 20th century.

The impressive interior represents a harmonious blend of Medieval and Renaissance styles, with a lofty triple nave, graceful arches, 29 side chapels and an intricately carved choir. Beneath the main altar is the crypt of Santa Eulàlia (the patron saint of Barcelona), which contains her tomb.

The 14th-century cloister is undoubtedly the most beautiful part of the cathedral, its garden of magnolias, palms and fountains making a cool retreat from the heat of urban Barcelona. There is even a small pond, with a flock of white geese, supposedly symbolising Santa Eulàlia's virginal purity. A small **museum** just off the cloister shelters many of the cathedral's most precious treasures. Near the main entrance is the Chapel of Christ of Lepanto (formerly the Chapter House), which is widely considered to be the finest example of Gothic art in the cathedral. It contains the crucifix carried on board *La Real*, the flagship of Don Juan of Austria (➤ 41) during the famous Battle of Lepanto.

Despite its grandeur, the cathedral remains very much a people's church. Worshippers outnumber tourists and on Sundays, Barcelonans gather in Plaça de la Seu at noon to perform the *sardana*, a stately Catalan folk dance which symbolises unity (➤ 69).

Soaring arches in the great cathedral

TOP TEN

2
Fundació Joan Miró

This dazzling gallery pays homage to Joan Miró, one of Catalonia's greatest artists, famous for his childlike style and use of vibrant colours.

Vibrant colours typify Miró's work

The Miró Foundation was set up by Joan Miró in 1971, and is devoted to the study of his works and to the promotion of all contemporary art. The gallery – a modern building of white spaces, massive windows and skylights designed by Josep Lluís Sert – is itself a masterpiece and a perfect place in which to pursue the Foundation's aims. It contains some 200 Mironian paintings, 153 sculptures, nine tapestries, his complete graphic works and over 5,000 drawings, making it one of the world's most complete collections of this great master.

Fragment of the Tapis de la Fundació Joan Miró, Joan Miró © ADAGP, Paris and DACS, London 1998

Miró was born in Barcelona in 1893 and, apart from a brief spell in Paris, spent most of his life in the city developing his bold style of vigorous lines and intense primary colours. In 1956 he moved to Mallorca, and remained on the island until his death in 1983.

Highlights of the gallery include some of Miró's earliest sketches, the tapestry *Tapis de la Fundació* and a set of black-and-white lithographs entitled *Barcelona Series* (1939–44) – an artistic appraisal of the war years. The roof terrace and gardens contain several striking sculptures.

The Foundation also presents temporary exhibitions of modern art, contemporary music recitals (➤ 114) and a special permanent collection called 'To Joan Miró', with works by Ernst, Tàpies, Calder and Matisse among others, a touching tribute to the person and his work.

- 28C2
- Avinguda Miramar 71,
- Oct–Jun: Tue–Sat 11–7, Jul–Sep: 10–8; Thu until 9:30; Sun 10:30–2:30
- Café-restaurant (££)
- Espanya
- 61
- Excellent
- Expensive

17

TOP TEN

3
Montjuïc

✣ 28C1

🍴 Cafés and restaurants (£–££)

Ⓜ Espanya

🚌 13, 55, 61

🚋 Montjuïc funicular from Paral.lel Metro

✋ Free

↔ Anella Olímpica (➤ 32)

Few can resist the charms of the city's local hill, with its museums, galleries, gardens and other attractions set in an oasis of natural calm.

The history of Montjuïc, a 213m-high hill south of the city and the dominant feature of its coast and skyline, has been linked to the city's history since prehistoric times. The Romans later called it 'Jove's Mountain' but today it is called 'Mountain of the Jews', after an early Jewish necropolis here. The castle, standing on the bluff, dates from the 16th to 18th centuries and houses the **Museu Militar**, exhibiting collections of military weaponry and uniforms from different countries and periods.

Museums

📷 Museu Militar: 93 329 86 31; Museu Arqueològic: 93 423 21 49; Museu Etnològic: 93 424 64 02;

🕐 Tue–Sun, times vary

✋ Cheap; Museo Etnològic free first Sun of month

Above: *view of Montjuïc from the Columbus monument*

In 1929 Montjuic was venue for the International Expo. Today many of its buildings are filled with museums. The **Museu Arqueològic** and the **Museu Etnològic** typify the Expo's architecture, as does the Palau Nacional, home of the Museu Nacional d'Art de Catalunya (➤ 19, 54).

Beneath the Palau Nacional, Plaça d'Espanya marks the main entrance to the Expo with Venetian towers, and an avenue leading to Plaça de la Font Màgica – 'Magic Fountain' – a spectacular sight that always draws the crowds. The road continues up past the Pavello Barcelona (➤ 66–7) and the Poble Espanyol (➤ 22) to Fundació Joan Miró (➤ 17) and the Anella Olympica (➤ 32), venue for much of the 1992 Olympic Games.

4
Museu Nacional d'Art de Catalunya (MNAC)

Dominating the northern flank of Montjuïc, this imposing Neo-classical palace contains a treasure trove of Catalan art spanning several centuries.

The newly reopened National Museum of Catalan Art is one of the best museums of medieval art in the world. It is housed in an extravagant National Exhibition building, built as the symbol of the 1929 World Exhibition (➤ 22), and is currently undergoing renovation by architect Gae Aulenti, who also converted the Gare d'Orsay into one of Paris's foremost museums.

The MNAC boasts the world's most eminent Romanesque art collection, with stone sculptures, wood carvings, gold and silverwork, altar cloths, enamels and coins and a beautifully presented series of 11th- and 12th-century murals, carefully stripped from church walls throughout Catalonia and precisely reconstructed in apses, as if they were still in their original locations. The idea for this collection originated in the early 20th century when the theft of national architectural treasures in Catalonia was at its height, necessitating a church-led crusade to move some of the region's most precious treasures to a safe location.

The museum's Gothic collection forms a striking contrast with over 400 highly ornate retables and sculptures, including an extraordinary 15th-century Virgin in full flamenco dress. A somewhat fragmented collection of Renaissance and baroque paintings embraces works by Tintoretto, El Greco and Zurbarán. Once restoration work has been completed (projected for 2001), the museum will also contain the Museum of Drawings and Prints, the Numismatic Museum of Catalonia, the General Library of Art History and the Museu d'Art Modern (➤ 54), which is currently located in the Ciutadella Park.

- 28C2
- Palau Nacional, Parc de Montjuïc
- 93 423 71 99
- Tue–Sat 10–7 (Thu until 9); Sun and hols 10–2:30. Closed Mon
- Café-bar (£)
- Espanya
- 13, 27, 38, 55, 57, 61, 91
- Excellent
- Expensive
- Anella Olímpica (➤ 32)

The MNAC – a treasure house of Barcelonan history

TOP TEN

5
Museu Picasso

Museu Picasso draws thousands of vistors

This fascinating museum traces the career of the most acclaimed artist of modern times, from early childhood sketches to the major works of later years.

The Picasso Museum is the city's biggest tourist attraction. It contains one of the world's most important collections of Picasso's work and the only one of any significance in his native country.

Pablo Ruiz Picasso was born in Andalucia, but moved to the Catalan capital in 1895, aged 14. He was already an exceptionally gifted artist, and, by the time of his first exhibition in 1900, was well known. In 1904 he moved to Paris, but nevertheless remained in close contact with Barcelona.

The museum contains work from his early years, notably a series of impressionistic landscapes and seascapes, a portrait of his aunt, Tía Pepa (1896), notebook sketches and paintings of street scenes, including *Sortida del Teatre* (1896) and *La Barceloneta* (1897), and the menu for *Els Quatre Gats* (Four Cats) café (▶ 94). Other selected works are from the Blue Period (1901–4), the Pink Period (1904–6), the Cubist (1907–20) and Neo-classical (1920–5) periods, through to the mature works of later years. There are also 41 ceramic pieces donated by his wife, Jacqueline, in 1982, which graphically demonstrate the astonishing artistic development of this great master.

- ✝ 29E4
- ✉ Carrer Montcada 15–19
- ☎ 93 319 63 10
- ⏲ Tue–Sat and hols 10–8, Sun 10–3. Closed Mon
- 🍴 Café-restaurant (££)
- Ⓜ Jaume I
- 🚌 14, 17, 19, 36, 39, 40 45, 51, 57, 59, 64, 157
- ♿ Very good
- ✋ Expensive (free first Sun of month)
- ↔ Museu Tèxtil i d'Indumentària (▶ 57)

TOP TEN

6
Parc Güell

Deemed a failure in its day, Gaudí's eccentric hilltop park is now considered one of the city's treasures and a unique piece of landscape design.

The architectural work of Gaudí is inseparable from Barcelona, largely thanks to his relationship with the Güells, a family of industrialists who commissioned from him a number of works. For Parc Güell, Don Eusebi Güell, Gaudí's main patron, had grand ideas for a residential English-style garden city, with 60 houses set in formal gardens. Gaudí worked on the project from 1900 to 1914, but it proved an economic disaster: only three houses were completed, and the park became city property in 1923.

The park's main entrance is marked by two eccentric pavilions. A grand stairway, ornamented by a dragon fountain, leads to a massive cavernous space, originally intended as the marketplace. Its forest of pillars supports a rooftop plaza bordered by a row of curved benches, covered in multicoloured *trencadís* (broken ceramics).

Throughout the 20 hectares of Mediterranean-style parkland, there are sculptures, steps and paths raised on columns of 'dripping' stonework. Gaudí himself lived in one of the houses from 1906 to 1926. Built by his pupil Berenguer, it is now the Casa-Museu Gaudí (☎ 93 284 64 46) and contains models, furniture, drawings and other memorabilia of the architect and his colleagues.

- 47D4
- Main entrance: Carrer Olot
- 93 424 38 09
- Daily Nov–Feb 10–6, Mar and Oct 10–7; Apr and Sep 10–8; May–Aug 10–9
- Self-service bar
- Vallcarca (and uphill walk)
- 24, 25, 28
- Free
- Hospital de la Santa Creu i Sant Paul (➤ 45); Parc de la Creueta del Coll (➤ 65)

Sit on one of Europe's most unusual park benches

TOP TEN

7
Poble Espanyol

This charming Andalucian square is the centre piece of the Poble Espanyol

You can tour the whole of Spain in an afternoon here at Barcelona's 'Spanish Village', a remarkable showcase of regional architectural styles.

✛ 28B2

✉ Avinguda de Marqués de Comillas s/n

☎ 93 325 78 66

🕓 Mon 9AM–8PM; Tue–Thu 9AM–2AM; Fri & Sat 9AM–4AM; Sun 9AM–midnight

🍴 Plenty (£–££)

Ⓜ Espanya

🚌 13, 61

✋ Expensive

↔ Anella Olímpica (➤ 32); Fundació Joan Miró (➤ 17); Montjuïc (➤ 18); Museu Nacional d'Art de Catalunya (➤ 19); Pavelló Barcelona (➤ 66–7)

Built for the 1929 World Exhibition, the Poble Espanyol (Spanish Village) was intended as a re-creation of the diversity of Spanish regional architecture through the ages. It could easily have resembled a stage set or a theme park, but instead, the 115 life-sized reproductions of buildings, clustered around 6 squares and 3km of streets, form an authentic village, where visitors can identify famous or characteristic buildings ranging from the patios of Andalucia to Mallorcan mansions and the granite façades of Galicia.

Within the village are bars and restaurants serving regional specialities, and over 60 shops selling folk crafts and regional artefacts. Some are undeniably over-priced, but there are also some real finds (➤ 107).

The Museum of Popular Arts, Industries and Traditions and the Museum of Graphic Arts are also located here and every Sunday at midday, a festa enlivens the main square.

The Poble Espanyol was smartened up for the 1992 Olympics, with the introduction of 'The Barcelona Experience' (a half-hour audio-visual history of the city) and several new restaurants and bars, including the extraordinary Torres de Ávila (➤ 113), a trendy 'designer bar'-cum-nightclub, currently one of Barcelona's hottest night spots. Excellent flamenco shows can also be seen at the Tablao de Carmen (➤ 114).

TOP TEN

8
La Rambla

Sooner or later, every visitor joins the locals swarming day and night down La Rambla, the most famous walkway in Spain.

Life on Barcelona's most famous street is never dull

The name La Rambla, derived from *ramla* (Arabic for 'torrent'), serves as a reminder that in earlier times, the street was a sandy gully that ran parallel to the medieval wall, and carried rainwater down to the sea. Today's magnificent 18th-century tree-lined walkway, running through the heart of the old city down to the port, is the pride of Barcelona. The central promenade is split into various distinctive sections strung head-to-tail, each with their own history and characteristics, from the flower stalls along Rambla de les Flors to the birdcages of Rambla dels Ocells (Walk, ➤ 51). And it is said if you drink from the famous fountain (➤ 51) in La Rambla de Canaletes you are sure to return to the city.

Promenading La Rambla is never the same twice, changing with the seasons, by the day and by the hour. It's an experience eagerly shared by people from every walk of life – tourists, locals, bankers, Barça fans, artists, beggars, street-performers, newspaper-sellers, pickpockets, night-clubbers, students, lovers and theatre crowds – all blending together with the noise of the traffic, the birdsong, the buskers, and the scent of the flowers. Such is the significance of this promenade *par excellence* to the city, that two words – *ramblejar* (a verb meaning 'to walk down the Rambla') and *ramblista* (an adjective describing someone addicted to the act of *ramblejar*) – have been adopted in its honour.

✚ 29D3

🍴 Plenty (£–£££)

Ⓜ Catalunya, Drassanes, Liceu

🚌 14, 17, 18, 22, 24, 36, 57, 59, 64

⛴ Boat excursions from Moll de les Drassanes (➤ 110)

↔ Ciutat Vella (➤ 38–9); Drassanes and Museu Marítim (➤ 41); Mercat de la Boqueria (➤ 49); Palau Güell (➤ 57); Plaça de Catalunya (➤ 67); Plaça Reial (➤ 68–9)

❓ Sant Jordi (St George's Day) celebrations on 23 April (➤ 108, panel)

23

TOP TEN

9
La Sagrada Família

Opposite and below: *the Sagrada Família must be seen to be believed*

Big Ben, the Eiffel Tower... most cities have a distinctive monument. Barcelona has Gaudí's Sagrada Família, his, as yet unfinished, cathedral.

- 29E6
- Plaça Sagrada Família
- 93 455 02 47
- Daily Oct–Feb 9–6; Mar and Sep 9–7; Apr–Aug 9–8
- Sagrada Família
- 18, 19, 33, 43, 44, 48, 50, 51
- Few
- Expensive (additional charge for lift)
- L'Eixample (➤ 42–3); Hospital de la Santa Creu i Sant Pau (➤ 45)
- Crypt museum, lift and stairway into the towers

Antoni Gaudí, the internationally prestigious figure of Catalan architecture, started work on La Sagrada Família (Temple of the Holy Family) in 1882, and for the latter part of his life dedicated himself entirely to his great vision for Europe's biggest cathedral. His dream was to include three façades representing the birth, death and resurrection of Christ, and eighteen mosaic-clad towers symbolising the Twelve Apostles, the four Evangelists, the Virgin Mary, and Christ. On his untimely death in 1926 (➤ 14), only the crypt, one of the towers, the majority of the east (Nativity) façade, and the apse were completed. Ever since, the fate of the building has been the subject of often bitter debate.

With a further estimated 80 years of work (which would include the destruction of several buildings in Carrer Mallorca and Carrer Valencia), it seems that the Sagrada Família will probably never be more than a shell. Even as it stands today, it has become a world-wide symbol of Barcelona, one of the great architectural wonders of the world, and a must on every visitor's itinerary.

TOP TEN

10
Santa Maria del Mar

- 29E4
- Plaça de Santa Maria
- 93 310 23 90
- Daily 9–12:30, 4:30–8
- Barceloneta, Jaume I
- 14, 17, 40, 45, 51, 57, 59, 64, 157
- Good
- Free
- Museu Picasso (➤ 20); Palau de Mar (➤ 58)

Right and below: *Santa Maria epitomises Catalan Gothic architecture*

Barcelona's seaside cathedral is a Gothic triumph, built to demonstrate Catalan supremacy in Mediterranean commerce.

The 14th-century church of Santa Maria del Mar (St Mary of the Sea) is located at the heart of La Ribera (The Waterfront), the medieval city's maritime and trading district. This neighbourhood's link with the sea dates back to the 10th century, when a settlement grew up along the seashore outside the city walls, around a chapel called Santa Maria de les Arenes (St Mary of the Sands). During the 13th century, the settlement grew and became known as Vilanova de Mar. Its identity was eventually firmly established with the transformation of the tiny chapel into the magnificent church of Santa Maria del Mar, built on what was then the seashore, as a show of maritime wealth and power. Indeed, the foundation stone commemorated the Catalan conquest of Sardinia.

The church was built between 1329 and 1384 and has a purity of style that makes it one of the finest examples of Barcelona's Gothic heritage. The plain exterior is characterised by predominantly horizontal lines and two octagonal, flat-roofed towers. Inside, the wide, soaring nave and high, narrow aisles, all supported by slim, octagonal columns, provide a great sense of spaciousness. Sadly, the ornaments of the side chapels were lost when the city was besieged, once by Bourbon troops in 1714 and again during the Spanish Civil War. The resulting bareness of the interior, apart from the sculpture of a 15th-century ship that sits atop the altar, enables you to admire the church's striking simplicity without distraction.

What to See

Barcelona	28–77
Food and Drink	52–3
In the Know	74–5
Exploring Catalonia	78–90

Above: *chimney detail on Gaudí's Casa Mila*
Right: *street entertainer on La Rambla*

WHAT TO SEE

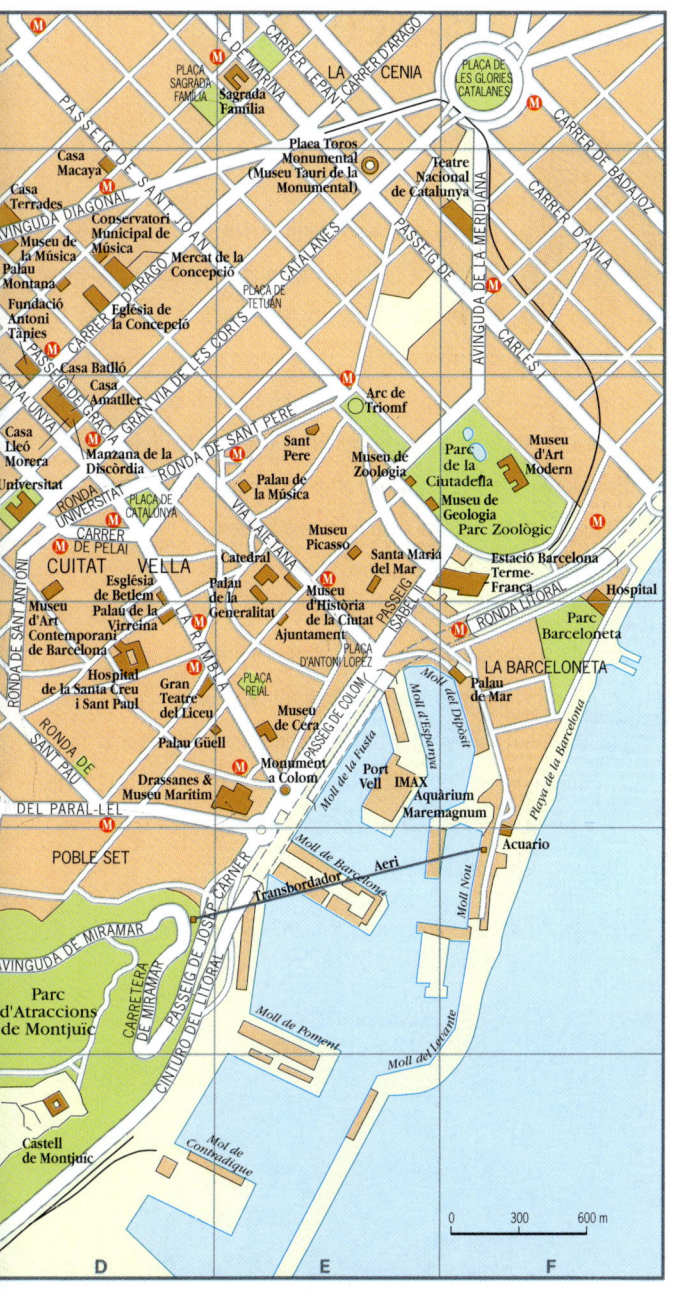

Barcelona

Ever since it was founded over 2,000 years ago, Barcelona has been striving to become a great metropolis. To its inhabitants, it is not Spain's second city but the capital of Catalonia; not a Spanish metropolis but a European one, and the Spanish leader in both *haute couture* and *haute cuisine*. The best time to see Barcelona in its true colours is after FC Barça wins an important match, and the streets erupt with excitement to the sound of car horns and popping champagne corks.

Visitors to Barcelona, on the other hand, are entranced by the Mediterranean atmosphere of the city, the richness of its art and architectural treasures both ancient and modern, the proud but not narrowly nationalistic character of the people, the strong tradition of theatre and music and the exuberant nightlife. In this dynamic and passionate city, it is easy to live life to the full, both day and night.

> *'I would rather be Count of Barcelona than King of the Romans.'*
>
> CHARLES V
> *Holy Roman Emperor (1519)*

BARCELONA

The City of Barcelona

Barcelona is easy to get to know. It is a compact city, small enough to explore on foot but great enough to be enormously varied. Most of the main sights are in three main areas: the Ciutat Vella (Old City), the Eixample and the Waterfront.

It is easy to lose yourself in the hidden corners of the Old City, to stumble upon a colourful market in a fountain-splashed square, to explore the city's boutiques, or to write some postcards in the geese-filled cloisters of the cathedral. The Eixample is particularly remarkable for the way the great turn-of-the-century Modernists (*Modernistas*) created some of the most imaginative and bizarre buildings in the world within the confines of a rigid grid system of streets.

The city has often been accused of ignoring the sea on which so much of its fame and prosperity has depended. The extension of the seafront began with the naming of Barcelona as host city for the 1992 Olympics. Today, with its smart coastal promenades, sandy beaches, and a plethora of open-air bars and restaurants, Barcelona's new image is 'Cara al Mar' ('Face to the Sea'). Leading from the seafront, La Rambla is a must for every visitor, a bustling avenue of cafés, bookstalls and flower kiosks, the best place to people-watch and to feel the true pulse of the city. By contrast, twin hills Montjuïc and Tibidabo provide a welcome refuge from downtown Barcelona, with their panoramic views over the rooftops to the Pyrenean mountains beyond and the sparkling Mediterranean sea.

Below: *on La Rambla*
Bottom: *Avinguda Portal de l'Angel.*

WHAT TO SEE

What to See in Barcelona

L'ANELLA OLÍMPICA

In 1992, Montjuïc mountain (► 18) was temporarily renamed 'Mount Olympus' and became Barcelona's main venue for the Olympic Games. Atop its western crest lies the Anella Olímpica (Olympic Ring), a monumental complex of concrete and marble that contains some of the city's most celebrated new buildings: Ricardo Bofills' neo-classical sports university, the Institut Nacional de Educació Fisica de Catalunya (INEFC); the Complex Esportiu Bernat Picornell swimming-pool complex; Santiago Calatrava's space-age communications tower, which dominates the skyline; and the remarkable black steel and glass domed Palau de Sant Jordi, designed by Japanese architect Arata Isozaki, which looks more like a UFO than a covered sports stadium.

Barcelona had bid for the games three times previously and had built Europe's biggest stadium for the 1929 World Exhibition with the clear intention of using it for the 1936 'People's Olympics' (organised as an alternative to the Nazi's infamous Berlin Games). These never took place due to the outbreak of Spanish Civil War the day before the official opening. For the 1992 games, local architects managed to preserve the stadium's original façade, while increasing the seating capacity from 25,000 to 70,000 by excavating deep into the interior. Today, highlights of the 1992 games can be relived through video clippings and souvenir showcases in the **Galería Olímpica**, located beneath the stadium.

- 34 C3
- Avinguda de l'Estadi/Passeig Olímpic, Montjuïc
- Estadi Olímpic: 93 481 10 92; Palau Sant Jordi: 93 481 01 92
- Espanya, or Paral.lel, then Funicular de Montjuïc
- 61
- Very good
- Free
- Montjuïc (► 18); Museu Nacional d'Art de Catalunya (► 19)

Galería Olímpica
- 93 426 06 60
- Apr–Jun: Tue–Sat 10–2, 4–7; (8PM Jul–Sep, 6PM Oct–Mar) Sun and hols 10–2.
- 61
- Good
- Cheap

Above: *the cable-car leading to Montjuïc, main venue of 1992 Olympics*

BARCELONA

LA BARCELONETA AND PORT OLÍMPIC ★★

Following the siege and conquest of Barcelona by Felipe V in 1714, a large area of the Ribera district was destroyed to make way for a new citadel (➤ 65, panel). The displaced residents lived for many years in makeshift shelters on the beach, until in 1755 a new district was developed on a triangular wedge of reclaimed land between the harbour and the sea, named La Barceloneta (Little Barcelona).

In the 19th century, La Barceloneta became home to seamen and dockers and it is still very much a working district, retaining its distinctive shanty-town atmosphere, fishy smells, and a quayside lined with the boats and nets of the local fleet. Today most visitors come here to eat in the many fine seafood eateries (*chiringuitos*), in particular those along the main harbourside thoroughfare, Passeig Joan de Borbó, and the restaurants of the converted Palau de Mar warehouse (➤ 58).

By contrast, Port Olímpic, with its smart promenades and glittering new marina, has given new impetus to Barcelona's nautical activities. Its chic restaurants, cafés and bars have become a lively night spot for both locals and tourists. Spain's two tallest buildings preside over the port – the office-filled Torre Mapfre and the five-star hotel Arts Barcelona, Barcelona's top hotel (➤ 101). Near by, a striking bronze fish sculpture (➤ 71, 74) by Frank Gehry (architect of the Guggenheim Museum in Bilbao) heralds the start of the Passeig Marítim, which links the port with La Barceloneta.

- 47 D1
- Barceloneta/Port Olímpic
- Plenty (£–£££)
- Barceloneta, Ciutadella/Vila Olímpica
- Barceloneta: 14,17, 36, 40, 45, 51, 57, 59, 64, 157. Port Olímpic: 10, 45, 57, 59, 71, 92, 157
- Parc de la Ciutadella (➤ 64); Port Vell (➤ 72); Vila Olímpica (➤ 73)

Hotel Arts and Gehry's 'Fish' – symbols of a new and progressive city

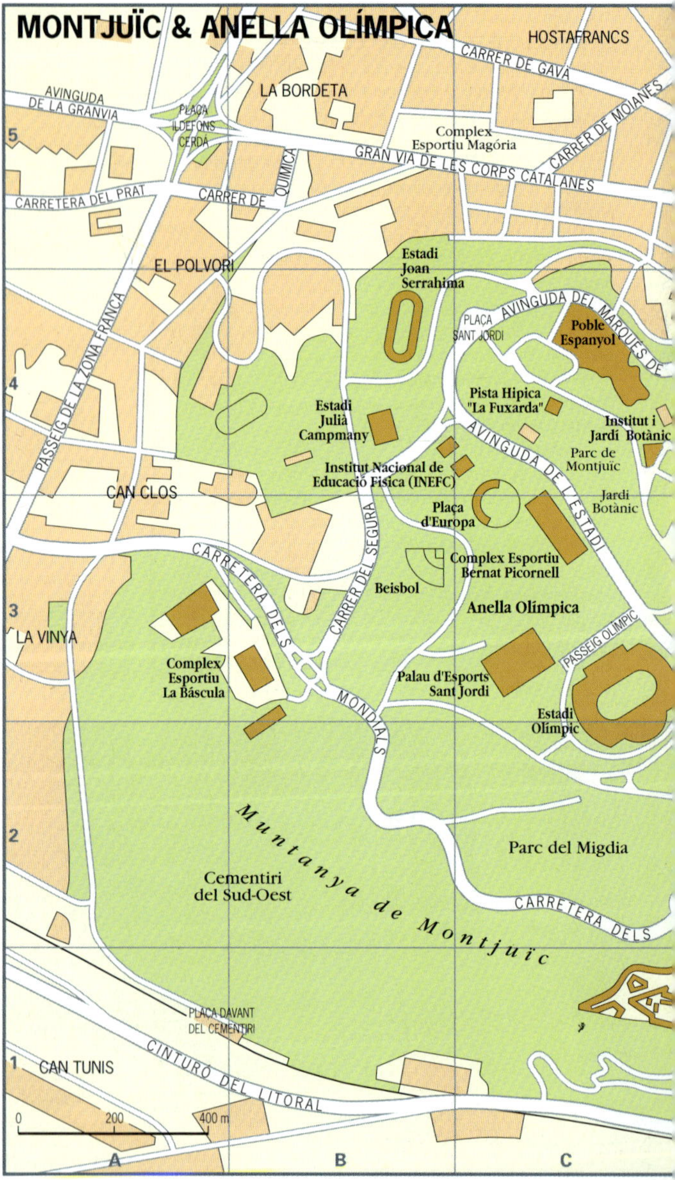
MONTJUÏC & ANELLA OLÍMPICA
HOSTAFRANCS
CARRER DE GAVÀ
LA BORDETA
AVINGUDA DE LA GRANVIA
PLAÇA ILDEFONS CERDÀ
Complex Esportiu Magória
CARRER DE MOIANÉS
GRAN VIA DE LES CORPS CATALANES
CARRETERA DEL PRAT
CARRER DE QUIMICA
EL POLVORI
Estadi Joan Serrahima
AVINGUDA DEL MARQUÈS DE
PLAÇA SANT JORDI
Poble Espanyol
PASSEIG DE LA ZONA FRANCA
Estadi Julià Campmany
Pista Hipica "La Fuxarda"
Institut i Jardí Botànic
AVINGUDA DE L'ESTADI
Parc de Montjuïc
Institut Nacional de Educació Fisica (INEFC)
CAN CLOS
Jardí Botànic
Plaça d'Europa
CARRETERA DELS MONDIALS
CARRER DEL SEGURA
Complex Esportiu Bernat Picornell
Beisbol
Anella Olímpica
LA VINYA
PASSEIG OLIMPIC
Complex Esportiu La Báscula
Palau d'Esports Sant Jordi
Estadi Olímpic
Muntanya de Montjuïc
Parc del Migdia
Cementiri del Sud-Oest
CARRETERA DELS
PLAÇA DAVANT DEL CEMENTIRI
CINTURÓ DEL LITORAL
CAN TUNIS
0
200
400 m
A
B
C
1
2
3
4
5

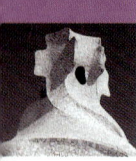

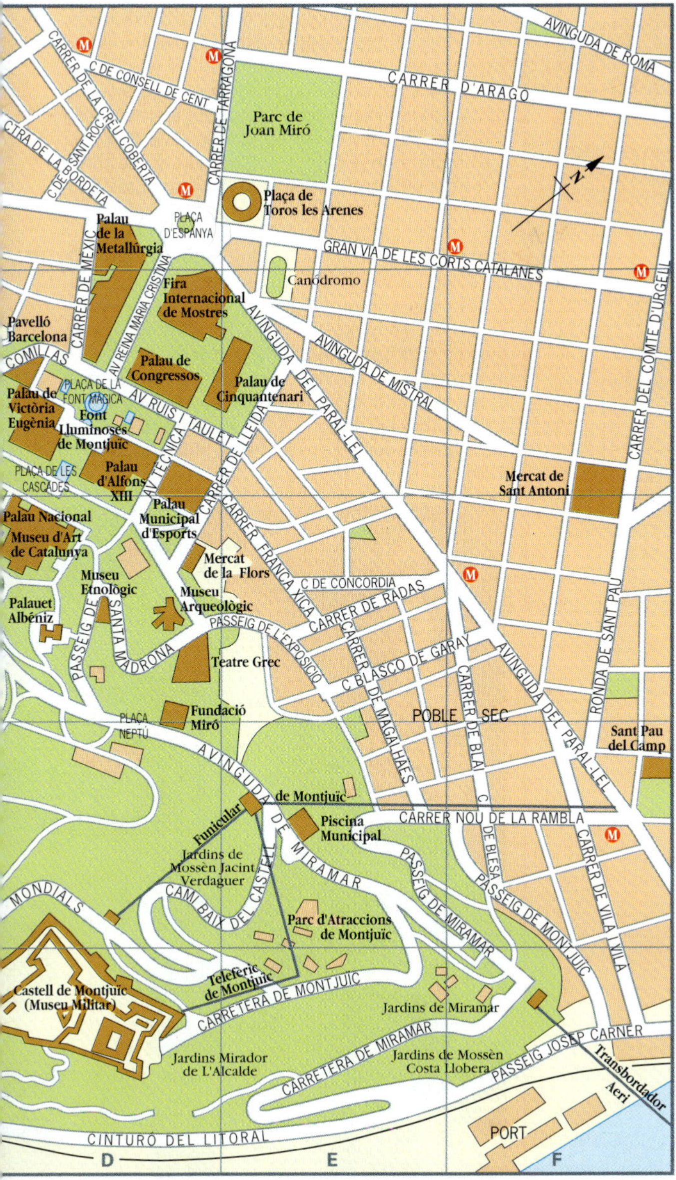
AVINGUDA DE ROMA
CARRER D'ARAGO
C DE CONSELL DE CENT
CARRER DE LA CREU COBERTA
CTRA DE LA BORDETA
C DE SANT ROC
CARRER DE TARRAGONA
Parc de Joan Miró
Plaça de Toros les Arenes
PLAÇA D'ESPANYA
N
Palau de la Metallúrgia
GRAN VIA DE LES CORTS CATALANES
Canódromo
CARRER DE MÉXIC
AV REINA MARIA CRISTINA
Fira Internacional de Mostres
Pavelló Barcelona
COMILLAS
Palau de Congressos
AVINGUDA DEL PARAL-LEL
AVINGUDA DE MISTRAL
CARRER DEL COMTE D'URGELL
PLAÇA DE LA FONT MÀGICA
Palau de Victòria Eugènia
AV RUIS I TAULET
Palau de Cinquantenari
Font Lluminoses de Montjuïc
PLAÇA DE LES CASCADES
Palau d'Alfons XIII
AV TÈCNICA
CARRER DE LLEIDA
Mercat de Sant Antoni
Palau Nacional Museu d'Art de Catalunya
Palau Municipal d'Esports
CARRER FRANCA XICA
Mercat de la Flors
C DE CONCORDIA
Palauet Albéniz
Museu Etnològic
Museu Arqueològic
CARRER DE RADAS
PASSEIG DE SANTA MADRONA
PASSEIG DE L'EXPOSICIÓ
CARRER DE MAGALHAES
C BLASCO DE GARAY
CARRER DE BLAI
RONDA DE SANT PAU
Teatre Grec
Fundació Miró
PLAÇA NEPTÚ
POBLE SEC
Sant Pau del Camp
AVINGUDA de Montjuïc
Funicular
Piscina Municipal
CARRER NOU DE LA RAMBLA
C DE BLESA
AVINGUDA DE MIRAMAR
Jardins de Mossèn Jacint Verdaguer
PASSEIG DE MIRAMAR
PASSEIG DE MONTJUÏC
CARRER DE VILA I VILA
MONDIALS
CAMÍ BAIX DEL CASTELL
Parc d'Atraccions de Montjuïc
Telefèric de Montjuïc
Castell de Montjuïc (Museu Militar)
CARRETERA DE MONTJUÏC
Jardins de Miramar
PASSEIG JOSEP CARNER
Transbordador Aeri
Jardins Mirador de L'Alcalde
CARRETERA DE MIRAMAR
Jardins de Mossèn Costa Llobera
PORT
CINTURÓ DEL LITORAL
D
E
F

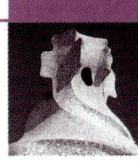

WHAT TO SEE

- 29 D4
- Passeig de Gràcia 41
- 93 216 01 75
- Mon–Fri 9–2
- Passeig de Gràcia
- Good
- Cheap
- Eixample (➤ 42–3); Fundació Antoni Tàpies (➤ 44)
- Only the entrance hall is open to the public

CASA AMATLLER

Chocolate manufacturer Antonio Amatller i Costa commissioned Josep Puig i Cadafalch to remodel Casa Amatller into an extravagant home with a neo-Gothic façade decorated with sculptures, coats of arms and floral reliefs, and crowned by a stepped gable. Inside the broad entranceway, the beautiful wooden lift was one of Barcelona's earliest elevators. Note also the amazing carvings on one interior doorway depicting animals making chocolate. There is a combined ticket (available from Casa Lleó-Morera, ➤ 37) for a guided tour of the three properties of Casa Amatller, Casa Batlló and Casa Lleó-Morera.

- 29 D4
- Passeig de Gràcia 43
- 93 216 01 12
- Interior not open to the public
- Passeig de Gràcia
- Good
- Cheap
- Eixample (➤ 42–3); Fundació Antoni Tàpies (➤ 44)
- Only the main staircase and roof terrace are open to the public

CASA BATLLÓ

Casa Batlló is one of the most famous buildings of the *Modernista* school, designed by Gaudí Josep Batlló i Casanovas and completed in 1907. It is said to illustrate the triumph of Sant Jordi (St George) over the dragon, with its mosaic façade, covered in glazed blue, green and ochre ceramics representing the scaly skin of the dragon, its knobbly roof the dragon's back, the tower the saint's cross, and the wave-like balconies the skulls and bones of victims.

Casa Batlló – Gaudí's famous 'dragon' building

BARCELONA

CASA LLEÓ-MORERA ✪✪

This striking *Modernista* building is considered Lluís Domènech i Montaner's most exuberant decorative work. Its flamboyant façade cleverly minimises the corner by placing visual emphasis on ornate circular balconies, columned galleries and oriel windows.

Inside, a florid pink mosaic vestibule and open staircase lead to the first-floor living quarters, lavishly decorated with stencilled stuccowork, stained glass, marquetry and mosaics, portraying roses (the nationalist symbol of Catalonia), lions (*lleó*) and mulberry bushes (*morera*).

- 29 D4
- Passeig de Gràcia 35
- No phone
- Interior not open to the public
- Passeig de Gràcia
- Good
- Cheap
- Eixample (➤ 42–3); Fundació Antoni Tàpies (➤ 44)

CASA MILÀ ✪✪

Known locally as La Perdrera (the quarry), Spain's most controversial apartment block and Antoni Gaudí's last and most famous secular building was built between 1906 and 1912 and shows this great Catalan architect at his most inventive. It also shows Gaudí's genius as a structural engineer, with seven storeys built entirely on columns and arches, supposedly without a single straight line or right-angled corner. Its most distinctive features are the rippling limestone façade, with its intricate ironwork, and the strangely shaped chimneys of the roof terrace.

After years of neglect, Casa Milà was declared a World Heritage site by UNESCO in 1984, and purchased by the Caixa Catalunya Foundation, which has invested over 8,000 million ptas to restore it to its original glory.

Although Casa Milà is now a World Heritage site, it so shocked Barcelonans when built that they nicknamed it 'La Pedrera' (the Quarry)

- 28 C5
- Passeig de Gràcia 92
- 93 484 59 80
- Tue–Sat 10–8; Sun 10–3. Guided tours: Mon–Fri 10, 11, 12, 1, 4, 5 and 6; Sat 10, 11, 12, 1; Sun: 11, 12, 1
- Diagonal
- Good (but not on roof)
- Expensive
- Eixample (➤ 42–3); Gràcia (➤ 44–5); Manzana de la Discòrdia (➤ 36–7); Sagrada Familia (➤ 24–5)

CATEDRAL (➤ 16, TOP TEN)

Did you know?

The Passeig de Gràcia between Carrer d'Aragó and Consell de Cent, containing Casa Amatller, Batlló and Lleó-Morera, is known as the Manzana de la Discòrdia *(Block of Discord), because of the clashing architectural styles.*

WHAT TO SEE

✚ 29 D4
🍴 Plenty (£–£££)
Ⓜ Jaume I, Liceu, Plaça de Catalunya, Urquinaona
↔ Plaça de Catalunya (➤ 67); Port Vell (➤ 72); La Rambla (➤ 23)

Explore the atmospheric lanes of the Ciutat Vella, a world away from the modern city

CIUTAT VELLA ✪✪✪

The tightly packed maze of narrow streets and alleyways of Barcelona's Ciutat Vella (Old City), bordered by the Ramblas, the Ciutadella Park, Plaça Catalunya and the sea, was once enclosed by medieval city walls and, until the massive building boom of the Eixample (➤ 42–3), 150 years ago, comprised the entire city.

At its heart is the Barri Gòtic (Gothic Quarter), one of several clearly identifiable *barris* or districts which make up the Old City. Its roots can be traced back to 1BC, when Roman soldiers established a small settlement called Barcino on a slight hill here called Mons Taber. This remarkable cluster of dark, twisting streets, quiet patios, sun-splashed squares and grand Gothic buildings was built inside the Roman fortifications, at a time when Barcelona, along with Genoa and Venice, was one of the three most important merchant cities in the Mediterranean and possessed untold riches. Its crowning glory, the Catedral (➤ 16), is surrounded by former residences of the counts of Barcelona and the Kings of Catalonia and Aragón. To the northwest lies Carrer Portaferrissa, the Old City's principal shopping street, with trendy boutiques and shopping arcades. To the south lies the spacious Plaça Sant Jaume (➤ 69) and a cobweb of narrow streets and interconnecting squares, including Plaça Sant Felip Neri, with its fine baroque church, Plaça del Pi, with its market of local produce and leafy Plaça Sant Josep Oriol, the 'Montmartre of Barcelona', where local artists display their works at weekends and buskers entertain the café crowds. Just off the square, the narrow streets bounded by Carrer Banys Nous, Call and Bisbe once housed a rich Jewish ghetto called *El Call*, but now the area is known for its antique shops.

As the city grew more prosperous in the early Middle Ages, new *barris*

BARCELONA

developed around the Roman perimeter, including La Mercè to the south and La Ribera to the east. The area south of Carrer de Ferran – La Mercè – is focused around the elegant, arcaded Plaça Reial (▶ 68–9) and the Church of La Mercè, Barcelona's patron Virgin. Though once very prosperous, this *barri* has become shabby and run-down, but is still worth exploring if only to seek out the excellent *tapas* bars along Carrer de la Mercè.

The *barri* of La Ribera, east of Via Laietana, holds much to interest the visitor. Its name (The Waterfront) recalls the time when the shoreline reached considerably further inland during Barcelona's Golden Age, when it was the city's main centre of commerce and trade and the favourite residential area of the merchant élite. Their handsome Gothic palaces still line its main street, Carrer Montcada. Several have since been converted into museums and galleries including Museu Picasso (▶ 20) and Libreria Maeght (▶ 107). The street leads to Santa Maria del Mar, the 'seaside cathedral' (▶ 26) and the Passeig del Born, with its popular restaurants, bars and craft shops.

Above: *tiled detail on a drinking fountain in the Barri Gòtic*
Below: *look for the ornate balconies and other hidden details above the shop fronts*

WALK

Barri Gòtic

Distance
2km

Time
1 hour (excluding visits)

Start/end point
Plaça Nova
✚ 41B3
Ⓜ Catalunya, Urquinaona

Coffee break
Mesón del Café (£)
✉ Carrer Llibreteria 16, just off Plaça Sant Jaume I
☎ 93 315 07 54

Leave Plaça Nova via the Portal del Bisbe (part of the Roman wall) into Carrer del Bisbe. Turn first left into Carrer de Santa Llúcia.

Note the tiny chapel of Santa Llúcia to your right, and the Gothic Archdeacon's House (Casa de l'Ardiaca) to your left. Just beyond is the main entrance to the Catedral (➤ 16).

From Plaça de la Seu, follow Carrer dels Comtes beside the cathedral, past Museu Frederic Marès (➤ 55). A left turn into Baixada de Santa Clara leads to Plaça del Rei (➤ 68). Return to the cathedral and skirt round its buttresses past the 14th-century Canon's House (Casa del Cánonges).

Stone plaques on the façade portray twin towers supported by winged goats with lions' feet, the heraldic symbols of medieval Barcelona.

Intricate stone lacework makes this bridge on Carrer del Bisbe unique

Turn sharp left, then left again onto Carrer del Bisbe, under a bridge and into Plaça Sant Jaume (➤ 69). Take Carrer de la Ciutat, then the first left until you reach Plaça Sant Just.

Here, the Església dels Sants Just i Pastor is reputedly the oldest church in Barcelona. Opposite, note the faded frescos on an elegant townhouse.

Leave the square along Carrer del Lledó. Turn first left then left again at the House of the Blue Tiles. Following the line of the Roman wall, cross Carrer Jaume I and continue up Carrer de la Tapineria, once the main street of medieval shoemakers.

Constructed between 270 and 310 AD, Barcelona's Roman walls were outgrown by the 11th century.

Continue along Carrer de la Tapineria past more Roman remains and return to Plaça Nova.

BARCELONA

DRASSANES AND MUSEU MARÍTIM ★★★

Barcelona's Museu Marítim (Maritime Museum) is located in the magnificent Drassanes Reials (Royal Shipyards), a splendid example of Gothic civil architecture. Since the 13th century, these impressive yards have been dedicated to the construction of ships for the Crowns of Catalonia and Aragon.

Today, their vast, cathedral-like, stone-vaulted halls contain maps, charts, paintings, pleasure craft and a huge range of other seafaring memorabilia chronicling the remarkable maritime history of Barcelona. The most impressive exhibit is a 60m replica of *La Real*, flagship of Don Juan of Austria, which forms part of an exciting 45-minute spectacle – 'The Great Sea Adventure'. Through headphones, visual and acoustic effects, visitors can experience life as a galley slave, encounter a Caribbean storm, join emigrants bound for the New World, and explore the seabed on board *Ictineo*, claimed to be the world's first submarine and built by Catalan inventor Narcís Monturiol.

- 29E3
- Avinguda de les Drassanes s/n
- 93 318 32 45/ 93 301 18 71
- Tue–Sun, 10–7. Closed Mon
- Café-restaurant (£)
- Drassanes
- Few
- Moderate
- Ciutat Vella (➤ 38–9); Monument a Colom (➤ 50); Port Vell (➤ 72); La Rambla (➤ 23)
- Library, bookshop, gift shop

Life on the ocean wave is explored in the Museu Marítim

- 28C5
- Plenty (£–£££)
- Catalunya, Diagonal, Entença, Girona, Hospital Clinic, Passeig de Gràcia, Provença, Tetuan, Vergaguer, Universitat
- Casa Milà (➤ 37); Fundació Antoni Tàpies (➤ 44); Manzana de la Discòrdia (➤ 36–7); Parc de Joan Miró (➤ 66); Sagrada Família (➤ 24–5)

L'EIXAMPLE ✪✪

L'Eixample means 'The Extension' in Catalan, and this district was laid out between 1860 and 1920 to expand the city beyond the confines of its medieval walls and to link it with the outlying municipalities of Sants, Sarrià-Sant Gervasi and Gràcia.

The innovative plan, drawn up by a liberal-minded civil engineer Ildefons Cerdà, broke completely with the tradition of Spanish urban planning, with its geometric grid of streets running parallel to the seafront, neatly dividing an area of 9sq km into 550 symmetrical blocks. The aptly named Avinguda Diagonal cuts through the rectilinear blocks at 45° to add a touch of originality. The utopian features of Cerdà's plan – such as gardens in the middle of each block and buildings on only two sides – have been largely forgotten, and today many people scorn the district for its monotony while others praise it as a visionary example of urban planning.

The Eixample is divided into two *barris*, either side of Carrer Balmes. *L'Esquerra* (The Left) is largely residential and of less interest to visitors whereas *La Dreta* (The Right) contains many of Barcelona's greatest *Modernistame* landmarks, including Casa Milà, the three properties of La Manzana de la Discòrdia, the Fundació Antoni Tàpies, the Hospital de la Santa Creu i Sant Paul, and the Sagrada Família. It is also a district of offices, banks and hotels. Chic boutiques and shops line its streets and, at night, Barcelona's smart set frequents its many restaurants, designer bars and discos.

Above: *Passeig de Gràcia, with its many shops, bars and restaurants, is one of the city's liveliest streets*

WALK

The Eixample District

This walk explores some of Barcelona's lesser-known examples of *Modernista* architecture.

Start in Plaça de Catalunya, and walk up Passeig de Gràcia.

This elegant avenue has its original wrought-iron street lamps with ceramic mosaic seats dating from 1906. Note Nos 6–14 (one of the last *Modernista* constructions), No 18 (the only surviving example of rationalist commercial architecture in Barcelona) and No 21.

Turn left at Casa Lleó-Morera (► 36–7), along Carrer Consell de Cent then first left into Rambla de Catalunya, past several contrasting Modernista *buildings (Nos 47, 54 and 77) until Diagonal. Turn right past Gaudí-influenced Casa Comalat at No 442 by Salvador Valery and continue until Puig i Cadafalch's Palau Quadras at No 373.*

This striking neo-Gothic building contains the Museu de la Música. Near by, UNESCO-listed Casa Terrades (Nos 416–20) is sometimes known as Casa de les Punxes ('House of Spikes') because of its steep gables and red-tiled turrets.

Turn right into Carrer Roger de Lluria, past Palau Montaner (Carrer Mallorca 278), an early work by Domènech i Montaner, and turn left into Carrer València, past Nos 285, 293, and 312, striking Modernista *buildings, and a large enclosed market. At Avinguda Diagonal, turn right.*

Don't miss the extraordinary undulating wooden façade of Casa Planells (No 332), by one of Gaudí's early collaborators, Josep Maria Jujol.

Turn left into Carrer Sicilia and continue on to the Sagrada Família (► 24–5).

Distance
4 km

Time
2–2½ hours (excluding visits)

Start point
Plaça de Catalunya
🚇 29D4
Ⓜ Catalunya

End point
Sagrada Família
🚇 29E6
Ⓜ Sagrada Família

Lunch break
Buy a picnic in the large, covered market (Mercat de la Concepció) to eat in Plaça Sagrada Família.
✉ Mercat de la Concepció, Carrer València

Above: *Casa Josefa Villanueva in Carrer València – one of the many* Modernista *buildings in the Eixample*

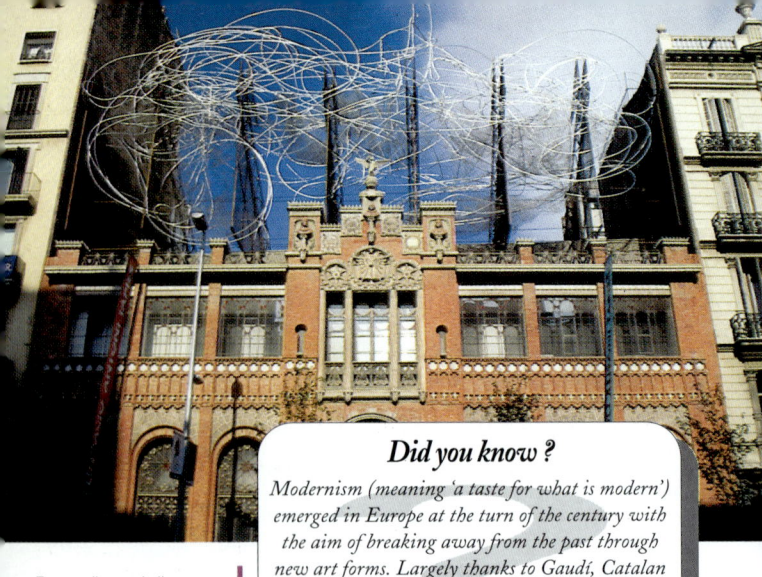

Extraordinary skyline – Fundació Tàpies' Cloud and Chair sculpture

Did you know?

Modernism (meaning 'a taste for what is modern') emerged in Europe at the turn of the century with the aim of breaking away from the past through new art forms. Largely thanks to Gaudí, Catalan Modernisme had the biggest impact, influencing all forms of European art, architecture, literature, and theatre, and making Barcelona an open-air museum of Modernism.

- 29D5
- Carrer d'Aragó 255
- 93 487 03 15
- Tue–Sun 11–8. Closed Mon
- Passeig de Gràcia
- Good
- Moderate
- Manzana de la Discòrdia (➤ 36–7, and panel)
- Library and small shop

FUNDACIÓ ANTONI TÀPIES ✪

The Tàpies Foundation was founded by Catalan artist Antoni Tàpies in 1984 to promote the study and understanding of modern art. It is housed in the former Montaner i Simon publishing house, built by Lluís Domènech i Montaner between 1880 and 1889, an unusual building that is considered the initiator of the Modernist movement. The striking *Mudejar*-style façade is crowned by an eye-catching tangle of wire and tubing by Tàpies, entitled *Cloud and Chair* (1990). Inside, there is an exhaustive library documenting art and artists of the 20th century, and one of the most complete collections of Tàpies' own works.

FUNDACIÓ JOAN MIRÓ (➤ 17, TOP TEN)

GRÀCIA ✪

- 28C6
- Plenty (£–£££)
- Fontana, Gràcia, Joanic, Plaça Molina
- Festa Major every August (➤ 116)

In 1820, Gràcia was a mere village of about 2,500 inhabitants. By 1897, the population had swollen to 61,000, making it the ninth-largest city in Spain, known as a radical centre of Catalanism and anarchism, still reflected in some street names – Mercat de la Llibertat and Plaça de la Revolució. Since then, Gràcia has been engulfed by the expanding metropolis, yet even now it maintains a village-like, no-frills, bohemian atmosphere and the *Graciencs* still call the cityfolk *Barcelonins*.

There are no real 'tourist' attractions here, except Gaudí's first major commission, Casa Vicens (✉ Carrer de les Carolines 24). Gràcia's real appeal is its muddle of narrow atmospheric streets and squares, and a concentration of reasonably priced bars, restaurants and popular night venues.

HOSPITAL DE LA SANTA CREU I SANT PAU ★★

This remarkable hospital complex is a masterpiece of *Modernisme* by innovative architect Lluís Domènech i Montaner. Not only did he deliberately defy the orderliness of the Eixample by aligning the buildings at 45 degrees to the street grid, but he also built the complex in contradiction to established hospital concepts by creating a 'hospital-village' of 48 small pavilions connected by underground passages and surrounded by gardens, rather than one single massive building.

Construction began in 1902, as a long-overdue replacement for the old hospital in the Raval, following a bequest from a Catalan banker called Pau Gil. The new hospital was inaugurated in 1930. The main pavilion, with its graceful tower and ornate mosaic façade, serves as a majestic entrance to the whole ensemble. Inside, the various pavilions are grouped around gardens that occupy an area equivalent to nine blocks of the Eixample, where both doctors and patients alike can enjoy a peaceful natural environment. The pavilions are decorated in ornate *Modernista* style using brick, colourful ceramics and natural stone. Over the years, the hospital complex has been restored several times and in 1984 it was declared a World Cultural Heritage site by UNESCO.

- 62A4
- ✉ Carrer de Sant Antoni Maria Claret 167–71
- ☎ 93 291 90 00
- 🍴 Small coffee shop in one of the pavilions (£)
- Ⓜ Hospital de Sant Pau
- ↔ Gràcia (➤ 44); Parc Güell (➤ 21); Sagrada Familia (➤ 24–5)
- ❓ Please remember that this is a hospital and not a tourist attraction

The main hospital of the Eixample – more palatial than most!

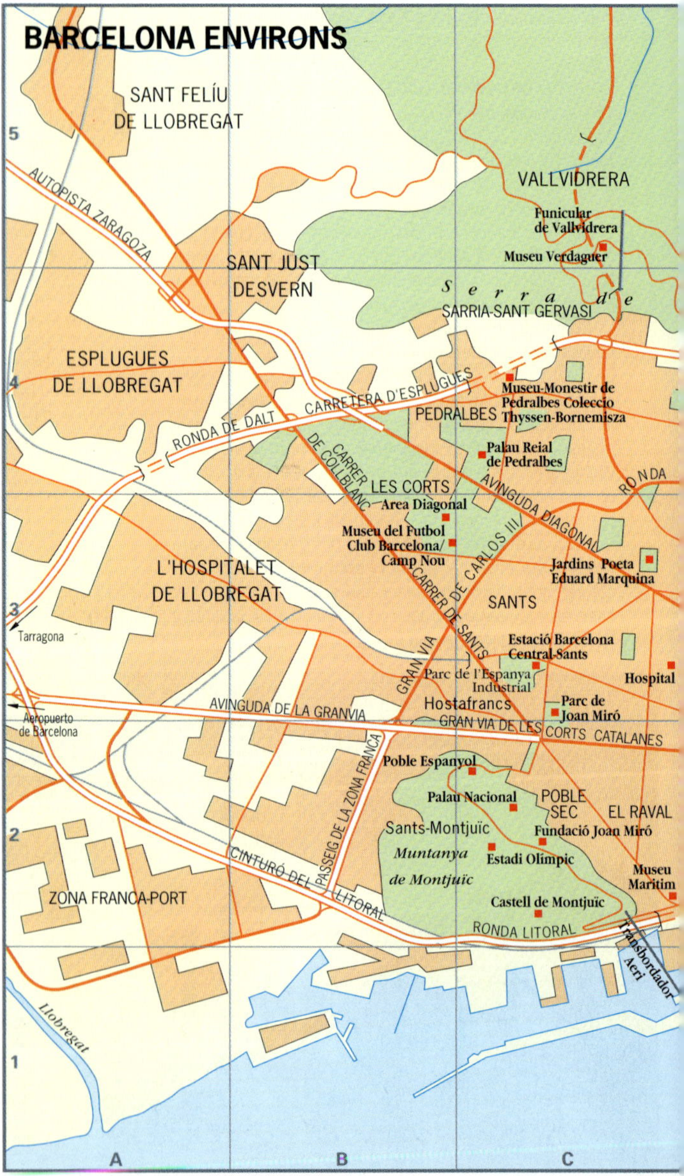
BARCELONA ENVIRONS
SANT FELÍU DE LLOBREGAT
AUTOPISTA ZARAGOZA
SANT JUST DESVERN
VALLVIDRERA
Funicular de Vallvidrera
Museu Verdaguer
Serra de
SARRIA-SANT GERVASI
ESPLUGUES DE LLOBREGAT
CARRETERA D'ESPLUGUES
Museu-Monestir de Pedralbes Coleccio Thyssen-Bornemisza
PEDRALBES
RONDA DE DALT
Palau Reial de Pedralbes
CARRER DE COLLBLANC
LES CORTS
AVINGUDA DIAGONAL
RONDA
Area Diagonal
Museu del Futbol Club Barcelona/ Camp Nou
CARRER DE CARLOS III
Jardins Poeta Eduard Marquina
L'HOSPITALET DE LLOBREGAT
CARRER DE SANTS
SANTS
Tarragona
Estació Barcelona Central-Sants
GRAN VIA
Parc de l'Espanya Industrial
Hospital
Hostafrancs
Parc de Joan Miró
AVINGUDA DE LA GRANVIA
GRAN VIA DE LES CORTS CATALANES
Aeropuerto de Barcelona
Poble Espanyol
PASSEIG DE LA ZONA FRANCA
Palau Nacional
POBLE SEC
EL RAVAL
Sants-Montjuïc
Fundació Joan Miró
Muntanya de Montjuïc
Estadi Olímpic
CINTURÓ DEL LITORAL
Museu Maritim
ZONA FRANCA-PORT
Castell de Montjuïc
RONDA LITORAL
Transbordador Aeri
Llobregat
5
4
3
2
1
A
B
C

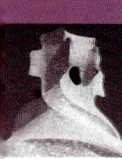

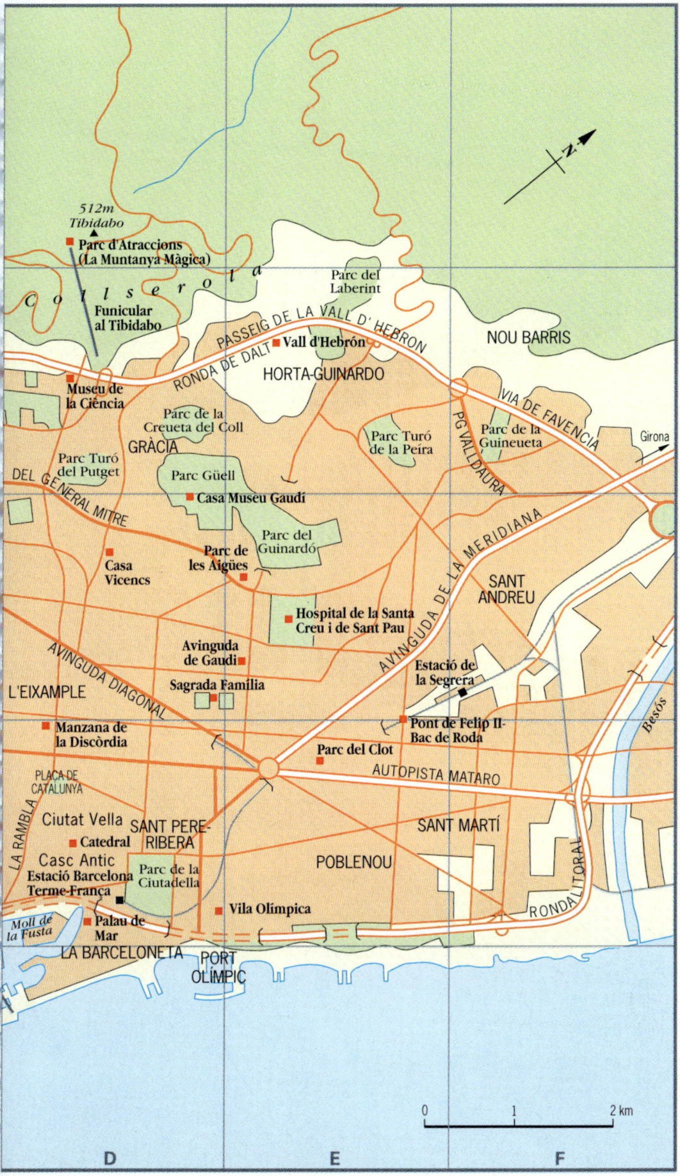

512m
Tibidabo
Parc d'Atraccions (La Muntanya Màgica)
C o l l s e r o l a
Funicular al Tibidabo
Parc del Laberint
PASSEIG DE LA VALL D' HEBRON
RONDA DE DALT
Vall d'Hebrón
NOU BARRIS
HORTA-GUINARDO
Museu de la Ciència
Parc de la Creueta del Coll
GRÀCIA
Parc Turó de la Peira
Parc de la Guineueta
VIA DE FAVENCIA
PG VALLDAURA
Girona
Parc Turó del Putget
DEL GENERAL MITRE
Parc Güell
Casa Museu Gaudí
Parc del Guinardó
AVINGUDA DE LA MERIDIANA
Casa Vicencs
Parc de les Aigües
SANT ANDREU
Hospital de la Santa Creu i de Sant Pau
Avinguda de Gaudí
Estació de la Segrera
AVINGUDA DIAGONAL
Sagrada Família
L'EIXAMPLE
Besòs
Manzana de la Discòrdia
Pont de Felip II-Bac de Roda
Parc del Clot
AUTOPISTA MATARO
PLAÇA DE CATALUNYA
LA RAMBLA
Ciutat Vella
SANT PERE-RIBERA
SANT MARTÍ
Catedral
Casc Antic
Parc de la Ciutadella
POBLENOU
RONDA LITORAL
Estació Barcelona Terme-França
Vila Olímpica
Moll de la Fusta
Palau de Mar
LA BARCELONETA
PORT OLÍMPIC
0
1
2 km
D
E
F

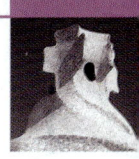

BARCELONA

MERCAT DE LA BOQUERIA 😊😊
Of more than 40 food markets in Barcelona, La Boqueria is the best and the busiest – always bustling with local shoppers, restaurateurs, gourmands and tourists. Its cavernous market hall (best entered through an imposing wrought-iron entranceway halfway up La Rambla) was built in the 1830s to house the food stalls that cluttered La Rambla and surrounding streets.

Inside is a riot of noise, perfumes and colours, with a myriad stalls offering all the specialities of the Mediterranean and the Catalonian hinterland – mouth-watering displays of fruit and vegetables, a glistening array of exotic fish, endless strings of sausages and haunches of ham, and sweetly scented bunches of herbs.

- 62A3
- Rambla 100
- 93 318 25 84
- Mon–Sat 7AM–8PM. Closed Sun
- Snack bars (£)
- Liceu
- Few
- Free
- Ciutat Vella (➤ 38–9); Drassanes and Museu Marítim (➤ 41); Plaça Reial (➤ 69); La Rambla (➤ 23); Gran Teatre del Liceu (➤ 114)

MONESTIR DE PEDRALBES AND COLLECCIÓ THYSSEN-BORNEMISZA 😊😊
The monastery of Pedralbes was founded by King Jaume II and Queen Elisenda of Montcada in 1326 to accommodate nuns of the St Clare of Assisi order. Following the king's death in 1327, Elisenda spent the last 37 years of her life here.

The spacious, three-storey cloisters – one of the architectural jewels of Barcelona – are still used by the Clarista nuns. Step inside and it is hard to believe you are just a short bus-ride from frenetic downtown Barcelona. From here, there is access to the refectory, the chapter house, the Queen's grave and St Michael's cell, with its remarkable wall murals.

Recently, Baron von Thyssen-Bornemisza donated part of his priceless art collection to the monastery, with 79 works housed in two former dormitories – mostly 13th- to 18th-century Italian and German paintings, including works by Fra Angélico, Lucas Cranach, Velázquez and Rubens.

- 46C4
- Baixada de Monestir 9
- Monastery: 93 203 92 82. Thyssen-Bornemisza Collection: 93 280 14 34
- Monastery and museums: Tue–Sun 10–2 5PM Sat). Closed Mon and hols. Church: Tue–Sun 10–1, 5:30–8:30, Mon 5:30–8:30
- 22, 63, 64, 75, 78,114
- Excellent
- Monastery: moderate. Thyssen-Bornemisza: moderate
- Palau Reial de Pedralbes (➤ 61)
- Bookshop

MONTJUÏC (➤ 18, TOP TEN)

Left: *the lively, colourful Mercat de la Boqueria*
Opposite: *enjoy a peaceful stroll through the Monestir de Pedralbes*

WHAT TO SEE

MONUMENT A COLOM ✪

This vast monument, commemorating the return of Christopher Columbus to Barcelona in 1493 from his first trip to the Americas, stands outside the naval headquarters of Catalonia, at the seaward end of the Ramblas. It was designed by Gaietà Buigas for the Universal Exposition of 1888, with Columbus standing at the top of a 50m column, pointing out to sea – towards Italy! Take the lift to the top for breathtaking bird's-eye views of the harbourfront.

- 62A1
- Plaça Portal de la Pau
- 93 302 52 24
- 10–2, 3:30–6:30, longer in summer and weekends.
- Drassanes
- Moderate
- Port Vell (➤ 72)

MUSEU D'ART CONTEMPORANI DE BARCELONA (MACBA) ✪✪

The new Barcelona Museum of Contemporary Art (MACBA), inaugurated in 1995, focuses on the art movements of the second half of the 20th century.

The museum building, itself a work of art designed by the American architect Richard Meier, has been the subject of much controversy but is increasingly being included as one of Barcelona's must-see landmarks. The vast white edifice with swooping ramps and glass-walled galleries almost upstages the works on display. Its location – surrounded by shabby old houses in the rundown district of Raval – is intended to spearhead investment in the neighbourhood.

MACBA's extensive collection (exhibited in rotation) covers the 1940s to the 1990s, with special emphasis on Catalan and Spanish artists. It contains works by Klee, Miró and Tàpies along with many others, including Joan Brossa, Maurizio Cattelan and Damien Hirst.

- 62A5
- Plaça dels Àngels 1
- 93 412 08 10
- 26 Sep–24 Jun: Mon, Wed–Fri 12–8; Sun and hols 10–9. Closed Tue. 25 Jun–25 Sep: Mon, Wed, Fri, Sat: 10:30–8; Sun and hols 11–7. Closed Tue
- Café (£)
- Catalunya, Universitat
- Excellent
- Expensive
- Ciutat Vella (➤ 38–9); La Rambla (➤ 23)

Above: *the Monument a Colom makes an impressive sight*

WALK

La Rambla

Start at Plaça Portal de la Pau, with your back to the sea and La Colom Monument (➤ 50), and head up the Ramblas, beginning at La Rambla de Santa Mònica. The convent here is the only 17th-century building still standing on La Rambla.

Distance
1km

Time
1 hour

Start point
Plaça Portal de la Pau
🕂 62A1
Ⓜ Drassanes

End point
Plaça de Catalunya
🕂 62B5
Ⓜ Catalunya

Coffee break
Café de l'Opera (➤ 98)
✉ Rambla dels Caputxins 47
☎ 93 317 75 85

This first section of Barcelona's famous street can be dangerous, especially at night, as it borders the Barri Xinès (China Town) district, renowned as a centre of drugs and crime. If you visit the Barri Xinès after dark, take a taxi.

Continue up to Plaça del Teatre and the Rambla dels Caputxins, on the site of an ancient Capuchin convent.

This was once the heart of the old theatre district, marked by a statue of Serafi Pitarra, 'father' of contemporary theatre in Catalonia. Today, only the shabby Teatro Principal remains.

Continue north past the Gran Teatre del Liceu (➤ 114) to Rambla de Sant Josep, which begins where the street widens, at Mercat de la Boqueria (➤ 49).

A meat market used to be held in the Plaça de la Boqueria. Indeed, 'boqueria' means 'butcher'. Today the square is decorated with a mosaic by Joan Miró. Flower-stands line this section, commonly called the Rambla de les Flors, whereas birds and other small creatures are sold in the Rambla dels Estudis, named after a university which once stood here, although now dubbed the Rambla dels Ocells (Boulevard of the Birds).

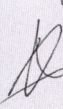

The final Rambla – La Rambla de Canaletes, named after its famous fountain (➤ 23) – leads to Plaça de Catalunya, the square where the city's heart beats fastest (➤ 67).

You can frequently find street artists in the Rambla dels Caputxins

FOOD & DRINK

Food & Drink

No one visiting Barcelona should leave without trying *la cuina Catalana*, its cuisine, described by the American food critic Colman Andrews as 'the last great culinary secret in Europe'. Rooted in the fresh local ingredients of the mountains, the plains and sea, the food is delicious and suprisingly subtle in flavour.

Mediterranean Flavours

The main ingredients of traditional Catalan dishes are typically Mediterranean: tomatoes, garlic, olive oil, aubergines, courgettes, peppers and herbs, which, when blended, form *samfaina*, a delicious sauce served with many dishes. Other principal sauces include *picada* (nuts, bread, parsley, garlic and saffron), *sofregit* (a simple sauce of onion, tomato and garlic lightly fried in olive oil) and *allioli* (a strong, garlicky mayonnaise).

For centuries pork (*llom*) has been the cornerstone of the Catalan diet. Little is wasted – even the *peus de porc* (pigs' trotters) are considered a delicacy. No bar would be complete without its haunch of *permil* (cured ham), a popular *tapas* dish (➤ 95 panel), and you often see a variety of sausages hanging from the rafters of restaurants and delicatessens. Lamb, chicken, duck, beef and game also feature strongly, often prepared *a la brasa* (on an open charcoal grill) and served with lashings of *allioli*.

Fresh fish is one of the gourmet delights of la Cuina Catalana

Mar i Muntanya

In Catalan cuisine, meat is commonly combined with fruit, creating such mouth-watering dishes as *pollastre amb pera* (chicken with pears) and *conill amb prunes* (rabbit with prunes). However, it is the unique 'surf'n'turf' combinations that sea and mountain (*Mar i Muntanya*) produce which differentiate *la cuina Catalana* from the cookery of other Spanish regions. *Sípia amb mandonguilles* (cuttlefish with meatballs) and *mar i cel* ('sea and heaven' – made with sausages, rabbit, shrimp and fish) are especially tasty.

FOOD & DRINK

Near the coast, fish dishes reign supreme, ranging from simple grilled *sardinas* (sardines) and hearty *sarsuela* (seafood stew) to eye-catching shellfish displays. Try *suquet de peix* (fish and potato soup) or the more unusual *broudegos* ('dog soup') made with fresh fish, onions and orange juice, followed by speciality dishes *arròs negre* (rice cooked in black squid ink), *fideuà* (a local variant of paella, using pasta and not rice) or *bacallà* (salt cod), which comes *a la llauna* (with garlic, parsley, tomato and white wine), *esqueixada* (in an onion, olive and tomato salad), *amb samfaina* or *amb romesco* (a piquant sauce, made from a mixture of crushed nuts, tomatoes and spicy red pepper).

Fine Wines

A short distance south of Barcelona, the Penedès is the main Catalan wine region, producing red (*negre*), white (*blanc*) and rosé (*rosat*) wines. Look for the reliable Torres, Masia Bach and René Barbier labels. Catalan *cava* (sparkling wine) also comes from the Penedès wineries, made by the *méthode champenoise* (➤ 113 panel). Famous names include Freixenet and Codorníu, which can be sampled in the champagne bars of Barcelona. To the north, the Alella and Empordà regions produce white wines, while Priorat produces excellent, heavy reds.

Visitors with a sweet tooth also find sustenance in Barcelona (➤ 96 panel)

Tasty tapas; tucking into portions of prawns and snails

MUSEU D'ART MODERN – MNAC ★★

The Museum of Modern Art shares a wing of the imposing Palau de la Ciutadella, with the Parliament of Catalonia, on the far side of the Parc de la Ciutadella (➤ 64). Its collections follow on from those of the National Museum of Catalan Art (➤ 19), completing a period spanning the 11th to 20th centuries, and are devoted to Catalan art from the mid-19th century to around 1930.

The collection starts with works by Maria Fortuny, the earliest of the *Modernistas* and the first Catalan artist to be known widely abroad, and friends Ramon Casas, whose work once hung on the walls of Els Quatre Gats (➤ 94), and Santiago Rusinyol. However, the highlight of the museum is, without doubt, its decorative arts collection: jewellery, textiles, stained glass, ironwork, sculptures, ceramics and painted screens by Homar, Puig I Cadafalch and Gaudí, among others.

The extravagance of *Modernisme* was succeeded by the less adventurous *Noucentisme* movement, which attempted to reintroduce the more harmonious values of Classical and Mediterranean art, epitomised by the works of Casanovas and Sunyer. The fascinating exhibition draws to a close with a series of striking avant-garde sculptures by Gargallo and Juli González, dating from the 1920s and 30s.

- 46B3
- Plaça d'Armes, Parc de la Ciutadella
- 93 319 57 28
- Tue–Sat 10–7; Sun and hols 10–2:30. Closed Mon
- Arc de Triomf, Barceloneta
- Good
- Moderate
- Barceloneta (➤ 33); Palau de Mar (➤ 58); Parc de la Ciutadella (➤ 64)

Above: *entrance to the Museu d'Art Modern*

Did you know?

FC Barcelona, or Barça for short, is more than Spain's top football club, the fifth most successful business in Spain, and the richest sports club in the world. During the Franco era, it stood as a Catalan symbol around which people could rally, and this emotional identification still remains today. It also explains why this legendary club has the world's largest soccer club membership (over 100,000 members) and why the streets still erupt with ecstatic revellers following a win over arch-rivals, Real Madrid.

BARCELONA

MUSEU FREDERIC MARÈS ★

Entrance to this museum, founded by local sculptor Frederic Marès in 1946, is via a beautiful medieval courtyard, which was once part of the Royal Palace of the Kings and Queens of Catalonia and Aragon. The museum itself is divided into two main sections: the sculpture collection, featuring works from the pre-Roman period to the 20th century, and the 'Sentimental Museum', which portrays daily life from the 15th to 20th centuries through an astonishing assortment of household items. Highlights include the women's section (with collections of fans, parasols, hat pins and jewellery), the smoker's room, and the charming entertainments room, with its puppet theatres, wind-up toys and dolls.

- 62C3
- Plaça de Sant Iu 5–6
- 93 310 58 00
- Tue–Sat 10–5; Sun and hols 10–2. Closed Mon
- Summer café (£)
- Jaume I
- Few
- Moderate
- Catedral (➤ 16); Ciutat Vella (➤ 38–9); Museu d'Història de la Ciutat (➤ 56); Plaça del Rei (➤ 68); Plaça Sant Jaume (➤ 68–9)
- Library, shop

Religious imagery in the Museu Frederic Marès

MUSEU DEL FUTBOL CLUB BARCELONA ★★

If you can't get a ticket to see Europe's top football team in action, then at least visit the Barcelona Football Club Museum, the city's most visited museum after the revered Picasso Museum (➤ 20). Even those who loathe football can't help marvelling at the vast Nou Camp stadium, which seats 120,000 spectators. The museum, under the terraces, presents a triumphant array of trophies, photographs and replays of highlights in the club's history before leading you to the shop, where everyone can buy a club shirt, pen, scarf, badge, mug ...

- 63F2
- Nou Camp – Gate 14 Carrer Arístides Maillol
- 93 496 36 00
- Mon–Sat 10–6:30; Sun and hols 10–2
- Café (£)
- Collblanc, Maria Cristina
- Moderate

MUSEU D'HISTÒRIA DE LA CIUTAT ★★★

The Museu d'Història de la Ciutat (City History Museum) is responsible for researching, conserving and publicising Barcelona's heritage. It is split into several sections in various locations around the Plaça del Rei (➤ 68). To start, visitors can familiarise themselves with the earliest origins of the city by wandering around the underground walkways beneath the square which explore a vast area of excavations that have exposed the ancient Roman settlement of Barcino.

The main entrance to the museum complex is at the opposite end of the square, in Casa Padellàs, a medieval mansion which was moved here stone by stone when the Via Laietana was created in 1930. Inside, carefully chosen, thoroughly documented exhibits trace Barcelona's remarkable evolution through two thousand years of history from a Roman trading-post to a wealthy 18th-century metropolis. Climb to the lookout point high above the galleries for memorable views of the square and the old city.

Back in the square, a visit to the medieval buildings of the Palau Real Major (the Great Royal Palace ➤ 68), completes the tour of the museum.

MUSEU NACIONAL D'ART DE CATALUNYA
(➤ 19, TOP TEN)

MUSEU PICASSO (➤ 20, TOP TEN)

MUSEU TAURI DE LA MONUMENTAL ★

Even though bullfighting has never had a particularly passionate following in Catalonia, the Museu Tauri De La Monumental (Bullfighting Museum), located inside the Monumental Bullring, is undoubtedly one of Barcelona's more unusual museums, with its dazzling array of fancy capes and costumes, photographs, old bullfighting posters and the mounted heads of bulls.

- 62C3
- Plaça del Rei s/n
- 93 315 11 11
- Tue–Sat 10–2, 4–8, Jul–Sep, 10–8; Sun and hols 10–2.
- Jaume I, Liceu
- None
- Expensive (free 1st Sat afternoon of the month)
- Catedral (➤ 16); Ciutat Vella (➤ 38–9); Museu Frederic Marès (➤ 55); Plaça Sant Jaume (➤ 69)
- Information service, shop and guided tours

Above: *the entrance of the Museu d'Història de la Ciutat*

- 35E5
- Gran Via de les Corts Catalanes 749
- 93 245 58 03
- Apr–Sep, 10:30–2, 4–7
- Monumental
- Moderate
- Sagrada Família (➤ 24–5)

BARCELONA

MUSEU TÈXTIL I D'INDUMENTÀRIA ✪

The Museu Tèxtil i d'Indumentària (Textile and Clothing Museum) acts as a reminder of how, thanks to its thriving textile industry, Barcelona rose to prosperity in the 1800s. It occupies a beautiful 14th-century palace, in what would then have been the aristocratic heart of Barcelona.

The museum collections include textiles, tapestries, lace and clothes from medieval to modern times, with displays of textile machinery, dolls, shoes, and other fashion accessories.

- 63D2
- Carrer Montcada 12–14
- 93 310 45 16
- Tue–Sat 10–5; Sun and hols 10–2. Closed Mon
- Café–restaurant (£)
- Jaume I
- Good
- Moderate
- Museu Picasso (➤ 20)

PALAU GÜELL ✪✪✪

This extraordinary building, constructed in 1886–8 and declared a World Cultural Heritage site by UNESCO, was Antoni Gaudí's first major architectural project, commissioned by the Güell family.

The façade is particularly striking, with its twin arches leading into the central vestibule. Off the latter are various rooms decorated with *Modernista* fittings. A ramp leads down to the basement stables, constructed with bare-brick columns and arches. The rooftop terrace is a mixture of random spires, battlements and chimneys of differing shapes and sizes, decorated with coloured ceramic mosaics. Look closely and on one you will find a reproduction of Cobi, the 1992 Barcelona Olympics mascot.

Unfortunately, the Güell family did not live here long. In 1936, the palace was confiscated by Spanish Civil War anarchists, who used it as their military headquarters and prison.

- 29D3
- Carrer Nou de la Rambla 3–5
- 93 317 39 74
- Mon–Sat 10–2, 4–8. Closed Sun
- Liceu
- None
- Moderate
- Mercat de la Boqueria (➤ 49); Ciutat Vella (➤ 38–9); Plaça Reial (➤ 68); La Rambla (➤ 23)

Plaça de Toros Monumental – Barcelona's main bullring

- 47D2
- Plaça Pau Vila 3, Port Vell
- 93 225 47 00
- Tue–Thu 10–7; Fri, Sat 10–8; Sun and hols 10–2:30
- Rooftop café (£)
- Barceloneta
- Excellent
- Expensive
- Barceloneta (➤ 33); Museu Picasso (➤ 20); Museu Tèxtil i d'Indumentària (➤ 57); Port Vell (➤ 72); Santa Maria del Mar (➤ 26)
- Multimedia library, community programmes

The newly renovated Palau de Mar warehouse is renowned for its excellent seafood restaurants

PALAU DE MAR ★★★

Thanks to the influence of the Olympic Games, and the opening up of the old port as a leisure area, the Palau de Mar (Palace of the Sea) – an impressive late 19th-century warehouse – has recently been converted into offices, harbourside restaurants and the spectacular Museu d'Història Catalunya (Museum of Catalan History).

This is Barcelona's newest museum, opened in 1996. Some critics have dubbed it a 'theme park', because of its lack of original exhibits, but it is nevertheless a dynamic and stimulating museum, covering the history of Catalonia in an entertaining fashion, through state-of-the-art displays, films, special effects, interactive screens and hands-on exhibits – tread an Arab waterwheel, mount a cavalier's charger, drive an early tram, take cover in a Civil War air-raid shelter...

The museum is divided into eight sections, each presenting a thorough picture of the economy, politics, technology, culture and everyday life of Catalonia over the centuries: the region's prehistory, the consolidation of Catalonia in the Middle Ages, its maritime role, links with the Austrian Empire in the 16th and 17th centuries, its economic growth and industrialisation, the 1936 Civil War and the ensuing repression of Catalonia under Franco, through to the restoration of democracy in 1979. The insight this innovative museum provides makes it easier for the visitor to understand the complexities of this 'nation within a nation'.

BARCELONA

PALAU DE LA MÚSICA CATALANA ✪✪✪

In a city bursting with architectural wonders, the Palau de la Música Catalana (Palace of Catalan Music) – commissioned by the Orfeó Català (Catalan Musical Society) in 1904 and created by local architect Lluís Domènech i Montaner between 1905 and 1908 – stands out as one of Barcelona's greatest Modernist masterpieces and a symbol of the renaissance of Catalan culture.

The bare brick façade is highlighted with colourful ceramic pillars, fancy windows and busts of Palestrina, Bach, Beethoven and Wagner. The sculptural group projecting from the corner of the building symbolises popular song. A balcony runs around the building and the main structure is supported by ornate columns that form huge dramatic archways over the entrance.

The interior continues the ornamental theme with a profusion of decoration in the entrance hall, foyer and staircase – almost overpowering in its attention to detail. The *pièce de résistance*, however, must be the concert hall, with its exquisite roof (an inverted cupola made of stained glass), its sculptures, ceramics and paintings dedicated to musical muses (including Josep Anselm Clavé, the great 19th-century reviver of Catalan music), and its beautiful balconies and columns, designed to enhance the perspective of the auditorium.

It is hardly surprising that this is Barcelona's main venue for classical music, and home to its two official orchestras, the Liceu orchestra and the Orquestra Simfònica de Barcelona i Nacional de Catalunya (the OBC). It is a memorable experience to attend one of the weekly concerts; the acoustics are superb, and the surroundings are as pleasing as the music.

- 63D4
- Carrer de Sant Pere Més Alt 1
- 93 268 10 00
- Mon–Fri 10–5
- Jaume 1, Urquinaona
- Few
- Cheap
- Catedral (➤ 16); L'Eixample (➤ 42); Plaça de Catalunya (➤ 67)
- Early booking for concerts essential

The Palau de la Música Catalana is a feast for the eyes as well as the ears

WALK

The Pedralbes District

Distance
3km

Time
1 hour (excluding visits)

Start point
Palau Reial de Pedralbes
✚ 46C4
Ⓜ Palau Reial

End point
Monestir de Pedralbes
✚ 46C4
🚌 22, 63, 64, 75, 78

The cool cloisters of Monestir de Pedralbes provide some welcome shade from the midday sun

Start at the Palau Reial de Pedralbes (► 61). Walk eastwards along the Avinguda de la Diagonal past the Law School and turn left up Avinguda de Pedralbes.

After a short distance on the left is the former Güell Estate (No 15). Note Gaudí's extraordinary wrought-iron entrance gate, which represents a dragon. Today the buildings house La Càtedra Gaudí, an institution specialising in subjects connected with this famous architect.

Continue up Avinguda de Pedralbes until the T-junction. Branch left into Carretera d'Esplugues.

At No 103, the Church of Montserrat was commissioned in 1920 as a gift for the Monastery of Montserrat (► 83) for use as a monastic foundation. The bequest was refused, so the property became part of the bishopric of Barcelona in the 1960s.

Turn right in front of the church, up Carrer Abadessa Olzet, first left along Avinguda Pearson then right again up Carrer Miret i Sans as far as Carrer de Panama 21.

Here, near the corner (No 21), a charming medieval farmhouse underlines the former rural character of Pedralbes. By contrast, No 13, a magnificent *Modernista* mansion with a gleaming polychromatic tiled roof, reflects the wealth of this district.

The road turns into Carrer de Montevideo and passes behind the monastery of Pedralbes (► 49), hidden behind bougainvillaea-smothered walls and framed by the hills of Tibidabo beyond. A flight of steps leads down Baixada del Monestir, past a small, leafy square, to the main entrance.

PALAU REIAL DE PEDRALBES

The Palau Reial de Pedralbes (Royal Palace of Pedralbes) is the result of the conversion in 1919 of the ancient villa of Can Feliu into a residence to accommodate the Spanish Royal family during the International Exhibition of 1929. After 1939, it became Franco's residence on visits to the city and, after various subsequent uses by royalty and heads of state, was opened to the public in 1960. The geometric gardens were landscaped by Nicolau Rubió i Turduri, who integrated the existing trees into his design, and there is even a fountain by Gaudí.

Today the state rooms house two museums. The Museu de Ceràmica traces the development of Spanish ceramics from the 12th century onwards, and includes the 18th-century Catalan panels *La Cursa de Braus* (the Bullfight) and *La Xocolotada* (The Chocolate Party), together with works by Picasso and Miró. The Museu de les Arts Decoratives has an impressive collection of decorative arts that spans the early Middle Ages to the present day. Special emphasis is placed on 20th-century developments, from decorative *Modernisme* to such movements as Functionalism and Minimalism, which are both totally void of decoration. The exhibits include some unlikely objects such as coffee-grinders, ice trays and even a urinal!

Above: *of all the luxury mansions in Pedralbes, the Palau Reial is the finest*

- 46C4
- Avinguda de la Diagonal 686
- Museu de les Arts Decoratives: 93 280 50 24. Museu de Ceràmica: 93 280 16 21
- Tue–Sun 10–3. Closed Mon
- Palau Reial
- Museu d'Arts Decoratives: good. Museu de Ceràmica: few
- Museums: moderate (free 1st Sun of month). Gardens: free
- Monestir de Pedralbes and Collecció Thyssen-Bornemisza (➤ 49)
- Shop, library, guided visits, educational services

Did you know?

The Zona Alta consists of old villages like Pedralbes, Sarriá, Bonanova and Sant Gervasi. In the 19th century, Barcelona's wealthy would spend their summer months here, in magnificent houses with lush gardens. Along with Horta ('market garden') to the east, with its gentrified farmhouses, this is still the home of many upper middle class Barcelonans.

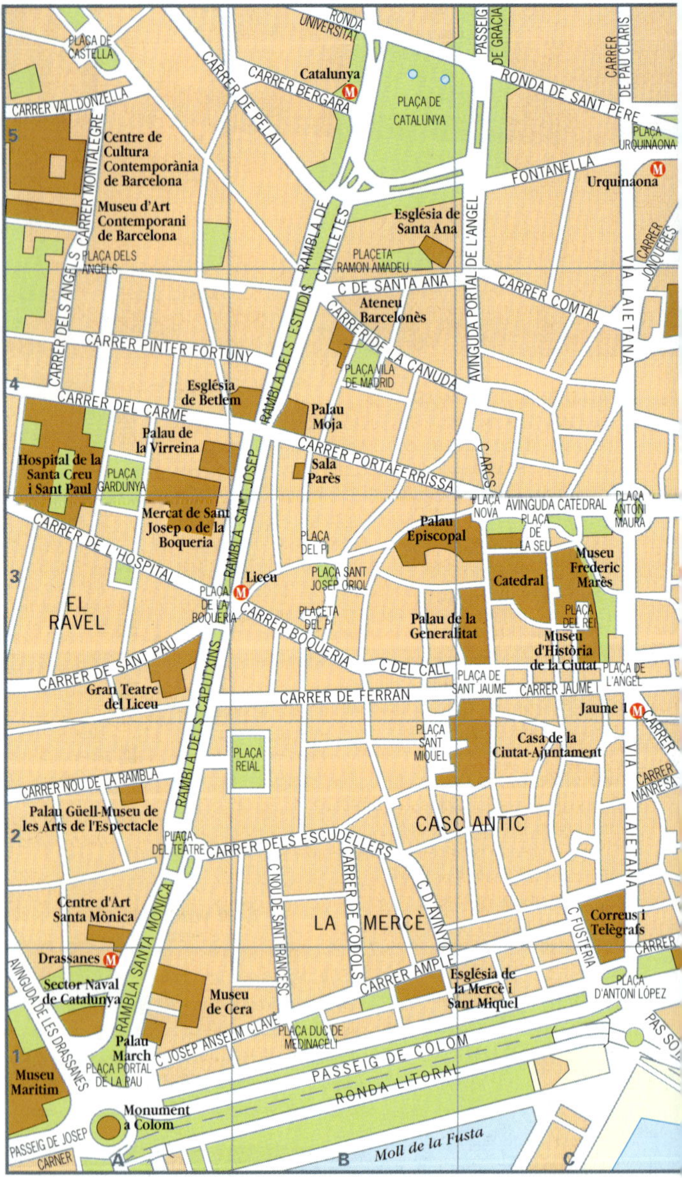

RONDA UNIVERSITAT
PLAÇA DE CASTELLA
CARRER DE PELAI
CARRER BERGARA
Catalunya
PLAÇA DE CATALUNYA
PASSEIG DE GRÀCIA
RONDA DE SANT PERE
CARRER DE PAU CLARIS
PLAÇA URQUINAONA
Urquinaona
FONTANELLA
CARRER VALLDONZELLA
Centre de Cultura Contemporània de Barcelona
CARRER MONTALEGRE
Museu d'Art Contemporani de Barcelona
PLAÇA DELS ÀNGELS
RAMBLA DE CANALETES
Església de Santa Ana
PLACETA RAMON AMADEU
C DE SANTA ANA
AVINGUDA PORTAL DE L'ANGEL
CARRER COMTAL
VIA LAIETANA
CARRER JONQUERES
CARRER DELS ANGELS
Ateneu Barcelonès
CARRER DE LA CANUDA
CARRER PINTER FORTUNY
RAMBLA DELS ESTUDIS
PLAÇA VILA DE MADRID
Església de Betlem
CARRER DEL CARME
Palau Moja
Palau de la Virreina
Hospital de la Santa Creu i Sant Paul
PLAÇA GARDUNYA
CARRER PORTAFERRISSA
Sala Parès
C ARCS
PLAÇA NOVA
AVINGUDA CATEDRAL
PLAÇA ANTONI MAURA
RAMBLA SANT JOSEP
Mercat de Sant Josep o de la Boqueria
PLAÇA DEL PI
Palau Episcopal
PLAÇA DE LA SEU
Museu Frederic Marès
CARRER DE L'HOSPITAL
Liceu
PLAÇA SANT JOSEP ORIOL
Catedral
PLAÇA DE LA BOQUERIA
PLACETA DEL PI
PLAÇA DEL REI
EL RAVEL
CARRER BOQUERIA
Palau de la Generalitat
Museu d'Història de la Ciutat
CARRER DE SANT PAU
C DEL CALL
PLAÇA DE SANT JAUME
CARRER JAUME I
PLAÇA DE L'ANGEL
Gran Teatre del Liceu
CARRER DE FERRAN
Jaume 1
RAMBLA DELS CAPUTXINS
PLAÇA REIAL
PLAÇA SANT MIQUEL
Casa de la Ciutat-Ajuntament
CARRER MANRESA
CARRER NOU DE LA RAMBLA
Palau Güell-Museu de les Arts de l'Espectacle
CASC ANTIC
PLAÇA DEL TEATRE
CARRER DELS ESCUDELLERS
C NOU DE SANT FRANCESC
CARRER DE CÒDOLS
C D'AVINYÓ
Centre d'Art Santa Mònica
LA MERCÈ
C FUSTERIA
Correus i Telègrafs
RAMBLA SANTA MONICA
Drassanes
CARRER AMPLE
Església de la Mercè i Sant Miquel
PLAÇA D'ANTONI LÓPEZ
AVINGUDA DE LES DRASSANES
Sector Naval de Catalunya
Museu de Cera
C JOSEP ANSELM CLAVÉ
PLAÇA DUC DE MEDINACELI
Palau March
PASSEIG DE COLOM
PLAÇA PORTAL DE LA PAU
Museu Maritim
RONDA LITORAL
Monument a Colom
PASSEIG DE JOSEP CARNER
Moll de la Fusta
A
B
C
1
2
3
4
5

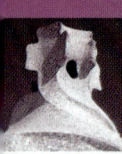

BARCELONA

CENTRAL BARCELONA

0 100 200 300 m

- Casa Calvet
- CARRER DE ROGER DE LLÚRIA
- CARRER DEL BRUC
- CARRER DE GIRONA
- CARRER DE BAILÉN
- PASSEIG DE SANT JOAN
- CARRER DE NÀPOLS
- CARRER D'AUSIÀS MARC
- RONDA DE SANT PERE
- CARRER D'ALIBEI
- CARRER D'ALIBEI
- C. D'ORTIGOSA
- CARRER DE TRAFALGAR
- C. MÉNDEZ NÚÑEZ
- CARRER DE TRAFALGAR
- CARRER DE ROGER DE FLOR
- CARRER DE RIBES
- Palau de la Música Catalana
- **Arc de Triomf** (M)
- AVINGUDA VILANOVA
- CARRER SANT PERE MÉS ALT
- Sant Pere
- PLAÇA SANT PERE
- Arc de Triomf
- CARRER REC COMTAL
- CARRER DELS ALMOGÀVERS
- CARRER SANT PERE MÉS BAIX
- PLACETA COMERÇ
- Palau Justicia
- LA RIBERA
- CARRER FONOLLAR
- AVINGUDA FRANCESC CAMBÓ
- CARRER PORTAL NOU
- PASSEIG LLUÍS COMPANYS
- CARRER BUENAVENTURA MUÑOZ
- Mercat Santa Caterina
- CARRER CARDERS
- PLAÇA SANT AGUSTÍ VELL
- C. TANTARANTANA
- CARRER DEL COMERÇ
- C. CORDERS
- PLAÇA PONS I CLERCH
- PASSEIG DE PUJADES
- CARRER DE LA PRINCESA
- Museu de Zoologia
- SANT PERE-
- Font Monumental
- Museu Tèxtil i de la Indumentària
- Museu Picasso
- CARRER DEL REC
- CARRER MONTCADA
- CARRER FUSINA
- Museu de Geologia
- Parc de la Ciutadella
- RIBERA
- ARGENTERIA
- PASSEIG DEL BORN
- PLAÇA COMERCIAL
- Mercat del Born
- PASSEIG DE PICASSO
- PLAÇA SANTA MARIA
- Església de Santa Maria del Mar
- C. CARRETES DEL BORN
- C. BONAIRE
- C. DE LA RIBERA
- Museu d'Art Modern
- PLAÇA D'ARMES
- Parlament de Catalunya
- CONSOLAT DE MAR
- Llotja
- PLAÇA DE PALAU
- AVINGUDA MARQUÈS DE L'ARGENTERA
- PASSEIG ISABEL II
- PASSEIG CIRCUMVAL·LACIÓ
- MURALLA
- Estació Barcelona Terme-França
- Parc Zoològic
- Barceloneta (M)
- PLAÇA DE PAU VILA
- RONDA LITORAL

PARC DE LA CIUTADELLA ✪✪

This delightful walled park is a haven of shade and tranquillity just a stone's throw from the old city and waterfront. What's more, hidden amongst the trees, lawns, promenades and a boating lake, lies the Parc Zoològic (➤ 111) and a host of other attractions.

In 1888 the park was the site of the Universal Exposition and still contains some impressive relics of that great fair, including a striking *Modernista* café which now houses the **Museu de Zoologia**, with highlights that include a fascinating Whale Room and a Sound Library of recordings of animal sounds.

Near by, the neo-classical **Museu de Geologia**, with its rare and valuable minerals, fossils and rocks, opened in 1878 as Barcelona's first public museum. The impressive Hivernacle greenhouse, originally built for the display of exotic plants, is today a popular café (➤ 98), and the arsenal of Felip V's citadel now houses the Museum of Modern Art (MNAC) (➤ 54). But the main showpiece of the park is the Font Monumental – a huge, neoclassical-style fountain, smothered in allegorical sculptures, which Gaudí contributed to as a student.

Outside the park on Passeig Lluís Companys, the monumental Arc de Triomf was constructed by Josep Vilaseca i Casanovas as the grand entrance to the Universal Exhibition.

- ✠ 63F2
- ✉ Main entrance: Passeig Lluís Companys
- Ⓜ Arc de Triomf / Barceloneta/Jaume I
- ♿ Good
- 🏛 Free
- ↔ Barceloneta (➤ 33)

Museu de Zoologia
- ✠ 63E3
- ✉ Passeig de Picasso
- ☎ 93 319 69 12
- 🕐 Tue–Sun 10–2
- 🏛 Moderate

Museu de Geologia
- ✠ 63E2
- ✉ Parc de la Ciutadella
- ☎ 93 319 68 95
- 🕐 Tue–Sun 10–2
- 🏛 Moderate

Did you know?

Ciutadella Park takes its name from the mighty citadel constructed here by Felip V, following his victory in the 1714 Siege of Barcelona (➤ 33). The people's hatred of this fortress and their continual protests led to its eventual demolition, and the creation of this large, leafy park in its place, which first opened to the public in 1869.

Above: *the imposing Font Monumental – Niagara meets Brandenburg Gate!*

BARCELONA

PARC DEL CLOT ✪
This park in the eastern suburbs has been built on the site of a disused railway yard and combines the walls and arches of the former rail buildings with a low-lying playing-field (the name 'Clot' in Catalan means 'hole') and a shady plaça, linked to a high grassy area of artificial hills and enigmatic sculptures by a lengthy overhead walkway.

- 47E2
- Carrer Escultors Claperós
- Jan, Feb, Nov, Dec 10–6; Mar and Oct 10–7; Apr and Sep 10–8; May–Aug 10–9
- Clot, Glories   Free
- Sagrada Família (➤ 24–5)

PARC DE LA CREUETA DEL COLL ✪
This new park was built in a disused quarry by Olympic architects Martorell and Mackay in 1987. Surrounded by dramatic cliff-faces, scattered with modern sculptures and embracing wooded pathways and a small sand-fringed boating lake, it serves the densely inhabited suburb of Vallcarca and is always packed in summer.

- 47D4
- Carrer Mare de Déu del Coll
- 10–6, 7, 8 or 9 according to season
- 25, 28, 87   Free
- Gràcia (➤ 44)

PARC DE L'ESPANYA INDUSTRIAL ✪✪
With works by many Catalan artists, this is Barcelona's most controversial park – a *nou urbanisme* project, built between 1982 and 1985 on the site of an old textile factory. It is built on two levels, the lower part comprising a large lake and grassy area, with steep white steps up to the much-scorned upper esplanade, where there are ten lighthouses, a series of water spouts and an immense metal play-sculpture entitled the *Dragon of St George*.

- 28B3
- Carrer Cicero
- Sants-Estació
- Free
- Montjuïc (➤ 18); Parc de Joan Miró (➤ 66)

The Parc de l'Espanya Industrial defies all traditional concepts of park design

PARC GÜELL (➤ 21, TOP TEN)

WHAT TO SEE

- 35E5
- Carrer Tarragona
- Snack bar
- Tarragona, Espanya
- Free
- Montjuïc (➤ 18); Parc de la Creueta del Coll (➤ 65)

Woman and Bird – centrepiece of Parc de Joan Miró

- 47E4
- Carrer Germans Desvalls, Vall d'Hebron
- Nov–Feb: 10–6; Mar and Oct: 10–7; Apr and Sep: 10–8; May–Aug 10–9
- 27, 60, 73, 76, 85
- Free

- 35D4
- Avinguda del Marquès de Comillas
- 93 423 40 16
- Apr–Oct: daily 10–8; Nov–Mar: daily 10–6
- 13, 61
- Good
- Cheap
- L'Anella Olímpica (➤ 32); Fundació Joan Miró (➤ 17), Montjuïc (➤ 18); Poble Espanyol (➤ 22)

PARC DE JOAN MIRÓ

This is one of Barcelona's most popular parks, occupying an entire city block on what was formerly the site of a massive abattoir, hence its nickname Parc de l'Escorxador (slaughterhouse). It was created in the 1980s, and is always full of people reading, jogging, dogwalking or playing *petanca* (boules) amidst the attractive pergolas and orderly rows of shady palm trees. The park's most famous feature, however, is a startling 22m-high sculpture by Joan Miró, covered in multicoloured ceramic fragments, named *Dona i Ocell* (Woman and Bird).

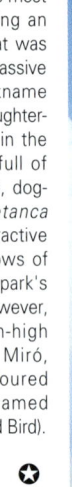

PARC DEL LABERINT

These romantic, Italian-style gardens, on the wooded outer rim of Barcelona near the Vall d'Hebrón, present a pleasing contrast to the stark modern *espais urbans* (urban spaces) of the city centre. They originally surrounded a grand 18th-century mansion, which has long since been demolished, but the park has maintained its formal flowerbeds, canals and fountains, its ornamental statuary and its centrepiece – the 'Labyrinth' – a beautiful topiary maze with a statue of Eros at its centre that has given the park its name.

PAVELLÓ BARCELONA

Bauhaus architect Ludwig Mies van der Rohe created this masterpiece of modern rationalist design for the 1929 Exhibition, a construction of astonishing simplicity and finesse in marble, onyx, glass and chrome, widely acknowledged as one of the classic buildings of this century. Astonishingly, it was dismantled at the end of the fair and subsequently meticulously reconstructed and reopened (in its original location) in 1986, on the centenary of Mies van der Rohe's birth.

Inside, take time to enjoy the quality of the colours, textures and materials, as well as a striking bronze sculpture entitled *Der Morgen* (The Morning) and the famous 'Barcelona' chair, a design of timeless elegance created especially for the Expo, which has since been copied world-wide.

BARCELONA

PLAÇA DE CATALUNYA

The Plaça de Catalunya is the heart of Barcelona and the hub of the city's transport system. It was first landscaped at the end of the 19th century and soon became of major importance as the pivotal point between the old and new city, with the Barri Gòtic (➤ 40–1) to the east, the carefully planned new Eixample district (➤ 42–3) to the north and west, and, to the southeast, La Rambla (➤ 23) running down to the port.

In 1927 the square was further developed, with the construction of hotels, restaurants and other important buildings. Its main landmarks today are the overpowering head office of Banco Espanol de Crédito, former headquarters of the unified Socialist Party of Catalonia during the Civil War; the monstrous El Corte Inglés department store (➤ 104, panel); and a medley of fountains and statues, including work by important sculptors such as Gargallo, Marès and Subirachs. Today, its benches, trees and splashing fountains make it a popular place to meet friends and have a coffee or simply to sit and soak up the Mediterranean sun.

- 62B5
- Plenty (£–££)
- Catalunya
- Ciutat Vella (➤ 38–9); L'Eixample (➤ 42–3); Palau de la Música Catalana (➤ 59); La Rambla (➤ 23)

Bird's-eye view of Plaça de Catalunya, a popular meeting point at the heart of the city

WHAT TO SEE

- 62C3
- Jaume I
- Catedral (► 16); Ciutat Vella (► 38–9); Museu Frederic Marès (► 55); Museu d'Història de la Ciutat (► 56); Plaça Sant Jaume (► 69)

Palau Reial Major
- 93 315 11 11
- Palace: Tue–Sat 10–2, 4–8; Sun and hols 10–2 Tower: Tue–Fri 10–2, 4–6
- Moderate

PLAÇA DEL REI ✪✪

The charming King's Square was once a bustling medieval marketplace. Today, it forms a frequent backdrop to summer open-air concerts and theatrical events, especially during the Grec festival (► 116), and is the location not only of the City History Museum (► 56) but also of the **Palau Reial Major** (Great Royal Palace), former residence of the Counts of Barcelona.

It was on the steps leading up to the Palau Reial Major that King Ferdinand and Queen Isabella are said to have received Columbus on his return from his first voyage to America in 1493. Inside, the Spanish Inquisition once sat in the Saló del Tinell, exploiting the local myth that should any prisoner lie, the stones on the ceiling would move. Today, the hall functions as an exhibition area.

On the north side of the square is the chapel of Santa Agata (also part of the royal palace), which contains a precious 15th-century altarpiece by Jaume Huguet. On the opposite side of the square, the Palau de Lloctinent (Palace of the Deputy) was built in 1549 for the Catalan representative of the king in Madrid. The strenuous climb to the top of its five-storey lookout tower (the Mirador del Rei Marti) is well rewarded by sweeping views of the old town.

The Palau Reial Major and St Marti's tower dominate the Plaça del Rei

BARCELONA

> ## *Did you know?*
> Catalonia's national folk dance, the sardana, is performed during summer, either in Plaça Sant Jaume (Sunday, 6–8PM) or in the Plaça de la Seu (Sunday, 10–midday; Wednesday 7–9PM). The dancers are accompanied by an instrumental group (cobla), which includes tenor and soprano oboes, a flabiol *(long flute)* and a tambori *(drum)*.

PLAÇA REIAL ✪✪

This sunny porticoed square, just off the Ramblas, with its tall palm trees, decorative fountain and buskers was constructed in 1848. Some of the façades are decorated with terracotta reliefs of navigators and the discoverers of America, and the two tree-like central lampposts mark Gaudí's first commission in Barcelona.

Keep a close watch on your belongings here – the square has a reputation for shady characters and pickpockets, hence the discreet but constant police presence. On Sunday mornings a coin and stamp market is held here.

- 62B2
- Plenty (£–££)
- Liceu
- Ciutat Vella (➤ 38–9)

PLAÇA SANT JAUME ✪

Once the hub of Roman Barcelona, this impressive square today represents the city's political heart, and is dominated by two buildings; the neoclassical and Gothic **Casa de la Ciutat** (Town Hall) and, directly opposite, the Renaissance **Palau de la Generalitat de Catalunya** (Government of Catalonia).

The origins of Barcelona's municipal authority date back to 1249, when Jaume I granted the city the right to elect councillors, giving rise to the creation of the Consell de Cent (Council of One Hundred). The famous Saló de Cent (Chamber of One Hundred) and the black marble Saló de las Cronicas (Chamber of the Chronicles) are among the architectural highlights of the Town Hall.

- 41B1
- Cafés (£)
- Jaume I
- Plaça del Rei (➤ 68)

Casa de la Ciutat
- 93 402 73 64
- Sat and Sun 10–2 or by special arrangement

Palau de la Generalitat de Catalunya
- 93 315 13 13
- Open for guided tours 23 Apr
- Free

POBLE ESPANYOL (➤ 22, TOP TEN)

Detail on the Palau de la Generalitat in Plaça Sant Jaume

WALK

The Waterfront

Start on Moll de les Drassanes near the Columbus Monument (► 50), then head along Passeig del Moll de la Fusta by the water's edge.

Once a timber wharf, this smart palm-lined walkway, together with the new Port Vell marina complex opposite (► 72), demonstrates how successfully the once-seedy waterfront has been redeveloped. Raised on stilts above the yacht basin, the Passeig de Colom is lined with lively bars and restaurants including Gambrinus, renowned for its rooftop lobster sculpture (► 74).

Continue walking northeast until Plaça d'Antoni López.

This busy square is dominated by the main post office (Correos y Telegrafos) and a notable mosaic sculpture by Roy Lichtenstein (► 74).

Above: *Lichtenstein's colourful mosaic sculpture,* Barcelona Head, *enlivens the waterfront*
Right: *Barcelona's waterfront is now a stylish place to be seen*

WALK

Leave the square via the arcaded walkway of Passeig d'Isabel II, past the Stock Exchange and the famous '7 Doors' (Set Portes) restaurant (► 95), and turn right at Pla de Palau. Cross the main road into La Barceloneta (► 33) and continue along the waterfront, past the Palau de Mar (► 58) with its fish restaurants, until you reach Passeig de Joan de Borbó.

Note the wide variety of architectural styles here, especially No 43, which is one of the best examples of 1950s architecture in Barcelona. To your right, the clock tower by the harbour was originally a lighthouse, and the Torre de Sant Sebastià on Moll Nou carries cable-cars, via the Jaume I Tower, to Montjuïc.

On reaching the seafront, turn left on to Passeig Marítim, which runs parallel to the beach all the way to the Port Olímpic, heralded by a massive, gleaming fish sculpture by Frank Gehry (► 33).

Distance
3 km

Time
2–3 hours (excluding visits)

Start point
Monument a Colom
🕇 29E3
🚇 Drassanes

End point
Port Olímpic
🕇 47D1
🚇 Ciutadella

Lunch break
Llevataps (££) (► 95)
✉ Palau de Mar, Plaça Pau Vila s/n
☎ 93 221 24 27

- 29E3
- Cafés, bars and restaurants (£–£££)
- Drassanes, Barceloneta
- Free
- Barceloneta (➤ 33); Drassanes and Museu Marítim (➤ 41); Palau de Mar (➤ 58–9); La Rambla (➤ 23)

Golondrinas
- Portal de la Pau
- 93 442 31 06
- Times of boat trips vary according to season (➤ 110)
- Drassanes
- Moderate

Above: *Port Vell Marina – one of the top anchorages of the Mediterranean*

PORT VELL ★★

Although Barcelona was founded on sea-going tradition, for many years its seafront was in decay, until a major redevelopment prior to the 1992 Olympics reintegrated the Port Vell (Old Port) into the city by transforming it into a lively new entertainment venue. The Rambla de Mar, a series of undulating wooden walkways and bridges, acts as an extension of La Rambla, connecting the city to Port Vell's many new attractions.

Maremagnum, Port Vell's biggest crowd puller, is a covered shopping and entertainment centre with smart boutiques, expensive restaurants, trendy bars, discos and fast-food joints. Adjacent to the conventional cinema complex, IMAX (➤ 110–11), the 'cinema of the future', shows spectacular films in three dimensions, with state-of-the-art wrap-around screens and sound. Near by, the Aquarium (➤ 110), one of the biggest and best in Europe, always proves popular with children.

Take a **Golondrina** (pleasure boat) for a different perspective of the new harbour developments. The luxurious leisure marina with over 400 berths in the previously derelict dockyard area is rapidly becoming one of the Mediterranean's most exclusive anchorages. Although the big ferries to the Balearics still depart from here, most commercial activity now takes place in the modern port further down the coast.

LA RAMBLA (➤ 23, TOP TEN)

SAGRADA FAMÍLIA (➤ 24–5, TOP TEN)

SANTA MARIA DEL MAR (➤ 26, TOP TEN)

BARCELONA

> ### Did you know?
> The name 'Tibidabo' is taken from the words uttered by Satan during his temptation of Christ in the wilderness, Haec omnia tibi dabo *(all these things will I give to you)*, si cadens adoraberis me *(if thou wilt fall down and worship me)'*.

TIBIDABO AND SERRA DE COLLSEROLA

The 550m-high Mont Tibidabo forms the northwestern boundary of Barcelona and boasts panoramic views over the entire city, and, on exceptionally clear days, Mallorca.

At its summit, and topped by a huge statue of Christ, stands the modern Church of the Secret Heart (Sagrat Cor), whose style is probably best described as 'neo-Gothic fantasy'. Near by, the 'Magic Mountain' **Amusement Park** (➤ 111) cleverly balances traditional rides with high-tech attractions on several levels of the mountaintop, and is always a fun day out for the family. Tibidabo is just one of the mountains of the Collserola range, a wonderful 6,550ha nature reserve with extensive woodlands full of wildlife. It is best reached by FGC train to Baixador de Vallvidrera. From here, it is a 10-minute walk uphill to the **information centre**, where details of clearly marked itineraries for walkers and cyclists are available.

- 47D5
- Cafés, snack bars (£–££)
- FGC Avinguda Tibidabo then Tramvia Blau to Plaça Doctor Andreu followed by the Tibidabo Funicular
- Free
- Museu de la Ciència (➤ 110–11)

Amusement Park
- Parc d'Atraccions del Tibidabo, Plaça Tibidabo 3–4
- 93 211 79 42
- Tue–Fri 11–7; Sat, Sun 11–9
- Funicular del Tibidabo
- Moderate per ride

Collserola Mountains Information Centre
- Centre d'Informació, Parc de Collserola
- 93 280 53 52
- daily 9:30–3. Closed 1 & 6 Jan, 25–26 Dec
- Baixador de Vallvidrera
- free

The 'Magic Mountain': Tibidabo's amusement park

VILA OLÍMPICA

The 1992 Olympic Games triggered a major renovation of Barcelona's maritime façade. Just behind the Port Olímpic, the run-down district of Poble Nou was developed into the Vila Olímpica – home to 15,000 competitors during the games, and now a high-tech corridor of apartment blocks, shops and offices.

- 47D2
- Vila Olímpica
- Plenty (£–£££)
- Ciutadella
- 36, 41, 71
- Museu d'Art Modern (➤ 54)

IN THE KNOW

In the Know

If you only have a short time to visit Barcelona and would like to get a real flavour of the city, here are some ideas:

10 Ways to Be a Local

Dress appropriately for Spain's most stylish city.
Learn a few words of Catalan and show interest in the regional culture.
Promenade on La Rambla (➤ 23).
Take a siesta.
Join Barcelonans for a *tertulia* (discussion) in a local café.
At weekends, visit a park or stroll along the waterfront promenades.
Follow the locals' time schedule.
Show interest in 'Barça', (➤ 54–5).
Join in the *sardana* regional dance (➤ 69).
Develop a taste for *pa amb tomàquet* (➤ 95, panel) and *allioli*. (➤ 52).

Try some tapas *beside Frank Gehry's* Fish *sculpture*

10 Top Street Sculptures

Fish, by Frank Gehry ✉ Hotel Arts, Passeig Marítim, Port Olímpica (➤ 33)
Barcelona Head, a giant mosaic sculpture by Roy Lichtenstein ✉ Passeig de Colom
Drac de la Font, Gaudí's famous 'Dragon of the Fountain' ✉ Parc Güell (➤ 21)
'La Ferralla' ('Scrap Iron'), the nickname given to the sculptural highlight of the Vila Olímpica ✉ Avinguda Icària
Gambrinus, a giant fibreglass lobster (➤ 71) by Xavier Mariscal ✉ Moll de la Fusta, Passeig de Colom
Landscape Sculptures by Beverly Pepper ✉ Parc de l'Estació del Nord
Wall by Richard Serra ✉ Plaça de la Palmera

Sardana Dancers outside the Montjuïc Funfair (➤ 110) ✉ Avinguda de Miramar
Donna i Ocell (Woman and Bird), in Parc Joan Miró (➤ 66) ✉ C. Tarragona
Nüvol i Cadira (Cloud and Chair) on the roof of Fundació Antoni Tapies (➤ 44) . ✉ C. Aragó 255

10 Top *Tapas* Dishes

Mandonguilles (meatballs)
Boquerones and anxoves (fresh and salted anchovies)
Calamarsos amb la sevtinta (small squid cooked in their ink)
Croquetes de pollastre, or ***de bacallá*** (croquettes with chicken or salt cod)
Empanats and ***empanadillas*** (pies and deep-fried pasties with tuna filling)

IN THE KNOW

Gambas al ajillo (prawns with garlic)
Faves a la Catalana (broad beans, onions and botifarra (blood sausage) cooked in white wine)
Pa amb tomàquet (white bread with tomato and olive oil)
Pescaditos (deep-fried whitebait)
Pops a la gallega (octopus with paprika and olive oil)

Top Markets

La Boqueria – fruit and vegetables market ⊙ Mon–Sat 7AM–8PM. Closed Sun ⓜ Liceu (➤ 49)

Concepció – fruit and vegetables in the Eixample ✉ C. Aragó ⊙ Mon–Sat 7AM–8PM. Closed Sun ⓜ Girona

Craft market ✉ Avinguda Pau Casals ⊙ first Sun of month from 10AM ⓜ Hospital Clinic

Els Encants – flea market ✉ Plaça de les Glòries ⊙ Mon, Wed, Fri, Sat from 8AM

Festa de Sant Ponç – annual market of honey, herbs, natural products ✉ Carrer Hospital ⊙ 11 May ⓜ Liceu

Plaça del Pi; honey, herbs, cheeses, cakes ⊙ first Fri and Sat of month 10AM;

La Boqueria – Barcelona's top market, just off La Rambla (➤ 49)

antiques ⊙ Thu from 9AM ⓜ Liceu

Plaça Reial – coins, stamps ⊙ Sun 10–2 ⓜ Liceu

Plaça Sant Josep Oriol – art ⊙ weekends only ⓜ Liceu

La Rambla – afternoon and evening craft market ⊙ Sat and Sun only ⓜ Drassanes

Ronda Sant Antoni – coins, books, postcards ⊙ Sun 10–2 ⓜ Universitat

Top Rides

Bus Turístic – a cheap way to see the main sights if time is limited (➤ 121)

Un Cotxe Menys – city tours by bicycle ✉ C. Esparteria 3 ☎ 93 268 21 05 ⊙ Tours: Sat & Sun 10AM–12:30, Tue and Sat 8.30PM–midnight

Golondrinas – pleasure-boat cruises around the harbour and the Olympic Port (➤ 72)

Telefèric – cable-car ride from Barceloneta to Montjuïc (➤ 18)

Tramvia Blau – Barcelona's last remaining tram grinds up the hill towards Tibidabo (➤ 73)

Top Views

Columbus Monument (➤ 50)
Parc Güell (➤ 21)
Mirador del Rei Martí (➤ 68)
Sagrada Família (➤ 24–5)
Torre de Collserola ☎ 93 211 79 42 ⊙ Wed–Sun 11–8

Passeig Colom from the Monument

WHAT TO SEE

Barcelona's Metro

Barcelona has an impressive and efficient underground rail system, enabling you to visit most places of interest quickly and conveniently, either by metro or by FGC train (▶ 121). Useful stations include Catalunya (for La Rambla), Barceloneta and Drassanes (for the waterfront), Jaume I (for the old city, the cathedral and Museu Picasso), Ciutadella for the Olympic port and village, and

BARCELONA

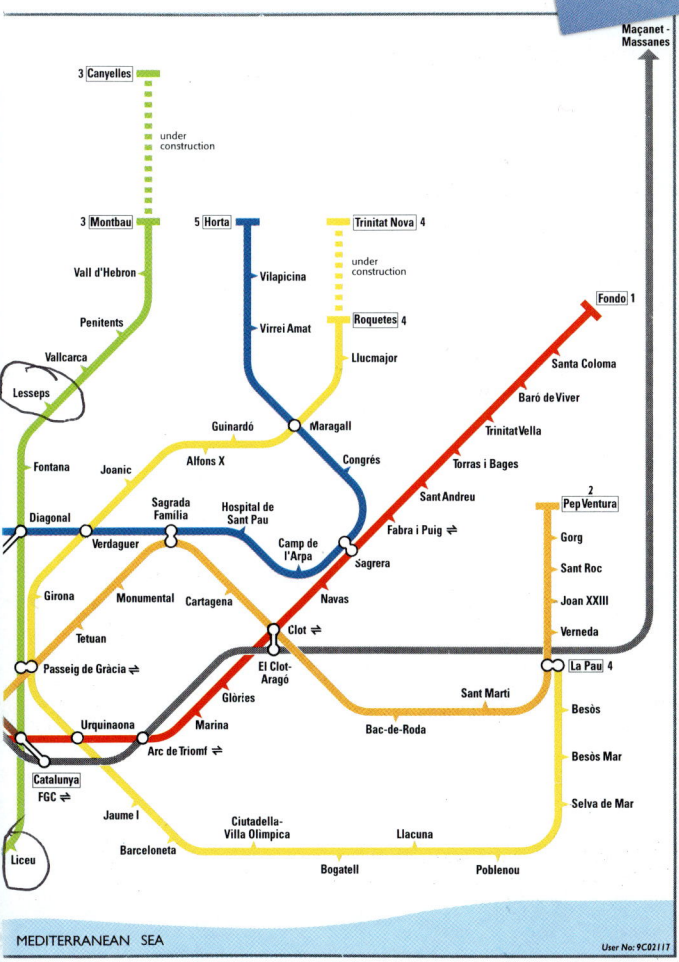

Passeig de Gràcia (for L'Eixample).

If you intend to use public transport frequently, buy one of several travelcards from any metro station or at any branch of La Caixa. The metro runs Mon–Thu 5AM–11PM; Fri, Sat and the evening before holidays 5AM–1AM; Sun 6AM–midnight. The FGC operates Mon–Thu 5:50AM–11PM; Fri–Sun 5:55AM–12:39AM.

Exploring Catalonia

It would be a shame to visit Barcelona without also seeing something of Catalunya (Catalonia). Despite being an autonomous province of Spain, this unique region feels in many ways like a separate country, with its own language and deeply rooted traditions, culture and cuisine. Its geographical location makes it the gateway to Spain. Over the centuries the passage of many peoples and civilisations has shaped the region, leaving magical cities such as Girona and Tarragona brimming with historical monuments, while its beautiful landscapes have provided inspiration for such artists as Gaudí, Miró, Dalí and Picasso.

The Catalan landscape is easy to tour, and offers a wide variety of scenery from the dramatic, snow-capped peaks of the Pyrenees and the secret bays and bustling fishing-ports of the Costa Brava, north of Barcelona, to the acclaimed Penedès vineyards and long golden beaches of the Costa Daurada to the south.

> '… the king, who had the sun for his hat (for it always shines in some part of his dominion), has nothing to boast of equal to Catalonia'
>
> PHILIP THIELENESSE,
> *A Year's Journey through France and Spain*, 1789.

The magnificent Catedral – pride of Tarragona

WHAT TO SEE

FIGURES

The main claim to fame of Figueres, two hours' drive northwest of Barcelona and just 17km from the Franco-Spanish border, is that the great Surrealist painter Salvador Dalí was born here in 1904 and gave his first exhibition in the town when he was just 14. In 1974, he inaugurated his remarkable **Teatre-Museu Dalí**, located in the old municipal theatre, and to this day it remains the most visited museum in Spain after the Prado in Madrid. It is the only museum in Europe that is dedicated exclusively to his works.

The building, topped with a massive metallic dome and decorated with egg shapes, is original and spectacular – in keeping with Dalí's powerful personality. Its galleries are housed in a number of enclosed, circular tiers around a

---

- 81D3
- Plaça del Sol ☎ 972 50 31 55
- Plenty (£–££)
- Girona (➤ 82)

Teatre-Museu Dalí
- Plaça Gala-Salvador Dalí 5
- 972 51 19 76
- Oct–Jun Tue–Sat 10:30–5:15; Jul–Sep daily 9–7:15; 26 Jul–31 Aug 10–00:30. Closed 1 Jan and 25 Dec
- None
- Very expensive

EXPLORING CATALONIA

CATALUNYA (CATALONIA)

central stage and a courtyard containing a 'Rainy Taxi' and a tower of car tyres crowned by a boat and an umbrella. The galleries contain paintings, sculptures, jewellery, drawings and other works from his private collection along with weird and wonderful constructions from different periods of his career, including a bed with fish tails, skeletal figures and even a complete life-sized orchestra. Dalí died in Figueres in 1989, leaving his entire estate to the Spanish State. His body lies behind a simple granite slab inside the museum.

Other sights in Figueres include over 3,000 exhibits in the famous **Museu de Juguets** (Toy Museum), set inside the old Hotel Paris, and the **Museu de l'Empordà** (Art and History), which provides an informative overview of the region's art and history.

Museu de Juguets
- La Rambla
- 972 50 45 85
- Mon–Sat 10–12:30, 4–7:30, Sun and hols 11–1:30, 5–7:30. Closed Tue (Sep–Jun) and Feb
- Moderate

Museu de l'Empordà
- La Rambla 1
- 972 50 23 05
- Tue–Sat 11–1, 3:30–7, Sun 11–2. Closed Mon
- Free

- 81D3
- Plenty (£–££)
- Figueres (▶ 80–1)

Catedral
- Plaça de la Catedral
- 972 21 44 26
- Daily 10–2, 4–7
- Good
- Free

Museu Arqueològic
- Esglesia Sant Pere de Galligans
- 972 20 26 32
- Summer: Tue–Sat 10:30–1:30, 4–7, Sun 10–2. Winter: Tue–Sat 10–2, 4–6, Sun 10–2
- Cheap

Banys Arabs
- Carrer Ferran Catolic
- 972 21 32 62
- Summer: Tue–Sat 10–7, Sun 10–2. Winter: Tue–Sun 10–2
- Cheap

Above: *Girona is one of the little-known gems of Catalonia*

GIRONA

Just 1½ hours by car or train from Barcelona, the beautiful, walled city of Girona is one of Catalonia's most characterful cities, with an admirable collection of ancient monuments. The old city, built on a steep hill and known for its lovely stairways, arcaded streets and sunless alleys, is separated from modern Girona by the River Onyar. The medieval, multicoloured houses overhanging the river are a photographer's dream, especially when seen from the iron footbridge designed by Eiffel. Most of the main sights are in the old city. Make sure you also allow time to shop along the beautiful Rambla de la Llibertat and to enjoy a drink in the arcaded Plaça de la Independencia.

At the heart of the old city, centred around Carrer de la Força, El Call, the old Jewish quarter, is one of the best preserved in Western Europe and is particularly atmospheric by night, with its street lanterns and intimate restaurants. Another splendid sight is the **Catedral**, with its impressive staircase leading up to a fine Baroque façade, a magnificent medieval interior and the widest Gothic vault in Europe. Housed inside another church, the **Museu Arqueològic** (Archaeological Musuem) outlines the city's history, and provides access to the Passeig Arqueològic, a panoramic walk around the walls of the old city. Near by, the 13th-century **Banys Arabs** (Arab Bathhouse), probably designed by Moorish craftsmen following the Moors' occupation of Girona, is the best preserved of its kind in Spain after the Alhambra, particularly striking for its fusion of Arab and Romanesque styles.

EXPLORING CATALONIA

MONTSERRAT

Fifty-six kilometres northwest of Barcelona, at the summit of Catalonia's 1,200m-high holy mountain, Montserrat– named after its strangely serrated rock formations (*mont*, mountain; *serrat*, sawed)– is one of the most important pilgrimage sites in the whole of Spain. Thousands travel here every year to venerate a medieval statue of the Madonna and Child called *La Moreneta* (The Black Virgin), blackened by the smoke of millions of candles over the centuries. The statue is said to have been made by St Luke and brought to the area by St Peter, and is displayed above the altar of the monastery church.

The spectacularly sited monastery, founded in 1025, is also famous for its choir, *La Escolania*, one of the oldest and best-known boys' choirs in Europe, dating from the 13th century. The choir sings daily at 1PM in the **Basilica**, a striking edifice containing important paintings including works by El Greco and Caravaggio.

Montserrat is clearly signposted by road from Barcelona, although the most enjoyable way to get there is by FGC train from Plaça d'Espanya, followed by a thrilling cable-car ride up to the monastery.

- 81C2
- Plaça de la Creu, Montserrat
- 93 835 02 51
- Limited choice of bars and restaurants

Basilica
- Monestir de Montserrat
- 8–10:30, 12–6:30
- Free

One of Spain's principal pilgrimage destinations – within easy reach of Barcelona

DRIVE

Alt Penedès

Distance
105km

Time
3–3½ hours (without stops)

Start point
Vilafranca del Penedès
✚ 81C2

End point
Sant Sadurní d'Anoia
✚ 81C2

Lunch break
🍴 Sant Jordi/Ca La Katy (££)
✉ 8½ km outside Vilafranca del Penedès
☎ 93 899 13 26

Vilafranca del Penedès
✚ 81C2
ℹ Carrer Cort 14
☎ 93 892 03 85
🍴 Plenty (£–££)

Sant Martí Sarroca
✚ 81B2
ℹ Plaça de l'Ajuntament 1
☎ 93 891 12 12
🍴 Limited choice (££)

The monastery of Santes Creus nestles among vineyards

The main attraction of this drive is its magnificent scenery. Leave Vilafranca del Penedès on the BP2121 past Mas Tinell, Romagosa Torné and Torres wineries (➤ 85), until you reach Sant Martí Sarroca after 9km.

This agricultural village contains an important Romanesque church with a splendid Gothic altarpiece, and a 9th-century castle.

Continue on to Torrelles de Foix with its tiled church dome. The road then climbs through barren scrub up to Pontons. Continue up past the Romanesque church of Valldossera, through Els Ranxox, over the Coll de la Torreta, to Santes Creus.

Santes Creus, founded in 1158 alongside the Gaia river, is one of three exceptional former Cistercian monasteries in the region (the others are Poblet and Vallbona de les Monges). Following its deconsecration, it grew into a small village in 1843 when a group of families moved into the abandoned buildings and monks' residences.

Turn right at the main road (TP2002) to El Pont d'Armentera. Join the T213 to Igualada. After 22km of breathtaking mountain scenery, turn right to La Llacuna, then left through farmland to Mediona. Continue to St Pere Sacarrera then turn right at the main road to St Quintí de Mediona. Several kilometres later, turn left to Sant Pere de Riudebitlles.

Mediona is noted for its medieval church and ruined castle while St Pere de Riudebitlles boasts a splendid Gothic manor house – the Palace of the Marquis of Lo.

The same road eventually leads to Sant Sadurní (➤ 85).

EXPLORING CATALONIA

PENEDÈS WINERIES – VILAFRANCA AND SANT SADURNÍ D'ANOIA

The Alt Penedès is one of Spain's most respected wine-producing areas, producing Catalonia's best-known wines and all of its *cava* (sparkling wine). Since ancient times, viticulture has been the main economic activity of its two main towns, Sant Sadurní d'Anoia and Vilafranca del Penedès.

Only half an hour's drive from Barcelona, Sant Sadurní is the centre of Catalonia's *cava* industry, with 66 *cava* firms dotted throughout the town. The largest, Codorníu, produces around 40 million bottles a year and its magnificent *Modernista* plant is open to visitors daily. Tours last 1½ hours and include a tasting.

Near by, Vilafranca del Penedès, the region's capital town, has more character than Sant Sadurní, with its fine arcaded streets and medieval mansions. In the Gothic quarter, surrounded by squares, palaces and churches, the **Museu del Vi** is the only museum in Spain to be wholly dedicated to wine. Current methods of production can be observed at Vilafranca's three top wineries – **Mas Tinell**, **Romagosa Torné** and **Miguel Torres** – all located just outside the town centre on the BP2121 to Sant Martí Sarroca.

Museu del Vi
- Plaça Jaume I, 1 and 3, Vilafranca del Penedès
- 93 890 05 82
- Tue-Sat 10–2, 4–7, Sun and hols 10–2. Closed Mon
- Cheap

Penedès Wineries
- Codorníu: 93 818 32 32; Caves Romagosa Torné: 93 899 13 53; Mas Tinell: 93 817 05 86; Miguel Torres: 93 817 74 87
- Opening times vary. Phone individual wineries for details

Did you know?

Penedès produces good red (negra or tinto), white (blanc) and rosé (rosat) wines. Of the many labels, René Barbier and Miguel Torres (the region's largest, most famous producer) are reliable, and dry Bach whites are also popular. Catalan cava is labelled according to quality and sweetness – Brut Nature, Brut, Sec, and Semi-Sec which, despite its name, is very sweet and the cheapest.

Above: *the Museu del Vi in Vilafranca*

WHAT TO SEE

✠ 81C2
ℹ Passeig de Vilafranca
☎ 93 894 12 30
🍴 Plenty (£–££)
↔ Costa Daurada (➤ 87); Tarragona (➤ 88–9)

Museums
✉ Cau Ferrat and Maricel de Mar: Carrer Fonolar; Romántic: Casa Llopis, Carrer Sant Gaudenci 1
☎ Cau Ferrat: 93 894 03 64; Romántic: 93 894 29 69
🕐 Tue–Sat 9:30–2, 4–6, Sun 9:30–2
♿ Few
✋ Cau Ferrat: moderate. Maricel de Mar and Romántic: cheap. Combined ticket available for all three museums
❓ Romántic: guided tours every hour

Museu Maricel de Mar houses an eclectic collection of Catalan treasures

SITGES ❂❂

Sitges, 40km south of Barcelona, is one of Spain's oldest bathing resorts and has long been the weekend and holiday playground of Barcelonans. It was once a sleepy fishing port and, although it has now developed into a thriving seaside destination, the old town still retains its ancient charm, with narrow streets, white-washed cottages and flower-festooned balconies. It also boasts several appealing *Modernista* buildings.

It was artist and writer Santiago Rusinyol who first put Sitges on the map, bringing it to the attention of artists such as Manuel de Falla, Ramon Casas, Nonell, Utrillo and Picasso. Rusinyol's house, **Cau Ferrat**, is today a museum, containing works by El Greco and Picasso amongst others. Neighbouring **Museu Maricel de Mar** houses an interesting collection of medieval and baroque artefacts, including Catalan ceramics, and the nearby **Museu Romántic** provides a fascinating insight into 18th-century patrician life in Sitges.

Sitges is famous for its beautiful Platja d'Or (Golden Beach), which stretches southwards for 5km from the baroque church of Sant Bartomeu i Santa Tecla. Its palm-fringed promenade is dotted with beach bars, cafés, and some of the coast's finest fish restaurants. However, the resort is perhaps best-known for its vibrant nightlife, drawing a young cosmopolitan crowd throughout the summer season. It is also a popular gay holiday destination. From October to May, Sitges is considerably quieter, except during *Carnaval* in mid-February when the town once more comes alive with wild parties and showy parades, drawing spectators from afar.

DRIVE

The Costa Daurada

The Costa Daurada (Golden Coast) takes its name from its long sandy beaches. This short drive starts in Tarragona and covers its northernmost stretch.

Leave Tarragona on the N340 coast road towards Barcelona. A few kilometres later you will arrive at the resorts of Altafulla and Torredembarra.

These two thriving holiday resorts attained great prosperity in the 18th century as a result of the wine trade with the American colonies. Note the Renaissance-style castle at Torredembarra.

Continue on the N340 for 6km. Turn left to Creixell.

The hilltop village of Creixell boasts a ruined medieval castle and a church with a striking *Modernista* belltower.

Return to the N340. After 2km, the road skirts the 2nd-century Roman Arc de Bara then continues to Coma-Ruga and Sant Salvador.

Coma-Ruga was once an area of marshland with mineral-water springs. At the turn of the century two spas were established around which this bustling resort developed. The local speciality, *xató* – a scrumptious cold fish salad, with a dressing similar to *romesco* (➤ 53) – must be sampled. At Sant Salvador, the cellist Pau Casals had his summer residence; today it is a museum.

From the Museu Pau Casals, the coast road leads to Calafell, where fishing boats are launched straight from the sand. Join the N246 here (direction Barcelona) and follow signs to Vilanova i la Geltrú.

The busy commercial centre of Vilanova is also a popular resort, thanks to its sandy beach, its palm-lined seafront, and its many appealing restaurants.

Continue on the N246 to Sitges (➤ 86).

Distance
63km

Time
1 hour (without stops)

Start point
Tarragona
✚ 80B1

End point
Sitges
✚ 81C2

Lunch break
🍴 Casa Victor (££)
✉ Passeig Maritim 23, Coma-Ruga
☎ 977 68 14 73

Long sandy beaches characterise the Costa Daurada

WHAT TO SEE

Tarragona

🕂 80B1
🍴 Plenty (£–££)
ℹ️ Carrer Major 39
☎ 977 242 52 03

This agreeable city is surprisingly undiscovered by most foreign visitors to the region, even though it contains the largest ensemble of Roman remains in Spain, the remarkable architectural legacy of Roman Tarraco, capital of an area that once covered half the Iberian peninsula. Originally settled by Iberians and then Carthaginians, it later became the base for the Roman conquest of Spain and the main commercial centre on this stretch of the coast until Barcelona and Valencia overshadowed it, after the Christian reconquest of Spain in the early 12th century.

The town is sited on a rocky hill, sloping down to the sea. The ancient upper town contains most of the Roman ruins, some interesting museums and an attractive medieval quarter with a grand cathedral. Below the Old Town lies the modern shopping district, centred on the Rambla Nova with its smart boutiques and restaurants, and a daily fruit and vegetable market in Plaça Corsini. Below the main town, the chief attraction of the lower part of the city is the maritime district of El Serrallo with its colourful fishing fleet, traditional *Lonja* (fish auction), and dockside restaurants that serve fish fresh from the nets. The rocky coastline beyond conceals a couple of beaches, notably Platja Arrabassada and Platja Llarga.

Catalan flags hanging in a Tarragona street

What to See in Tarragona

✉ Carrer Oleguer
🕐 Apr–Sep Tue–Sat 10–8, Sun 10–3; Oct–Mar Tue–Sat 10–5:30, Sun 10–3
♿ None
💰 Moderate (combined ticket)

AMFITEATRE ROMA

Built into the hillside overlooking the Mediterranean, the Amfiteatre Roma (Roman Amphitheatre) was where the Romans held their public spectacles, including combats between gladiators and wild animals before an audience of some 12,000 people. During the 12th century the Romanesque church of Santa Maria del Miracle was built on the site, giving the beach below its name – El Miracle. You can visit the Amfiteatre, Passeig Arqueològic, Museu d'Història, Circ Romà (▶ 90) and Casa Museu de Castellarnau (▶ 90) on a combined ticket.

Pause a while in the cool cathedral to admire its many treasures

CATEDRAL ★
Tarragona's grandiose Catedral – a magnificent Romanesque-Gothic building, in the form of a cross – was built as the centrepiece of the ciutat antiga (old city).

† 80B1
✉ Plaça de la Seu
🕐 Mon–Sat 10–1, 4–7; winter: 10–2

MUSEU ARQUEOLÒGIC AND MUSEU D'HISTÒRIA ★
The fascinating Museu Arqueològic (Archeological Museum) includes a section of the old Roman wall, statues of emperors, several sarcophagi and some interesting mosaics. Near by stands the Praetorium and the vaults of the 1st-century Roman Circus. The Praetorium is the site of the Museu d'Història (Tarragona History Museum), which traces the origins and history of the city through such treasures as the sarcophagus of Hipolitus, a masterpiece that was rescued from the sea in 1948.

† 80B1
✉ Plaça del Rei
☎ 977 24 57 96/ 977 24 19 52
🕐 Museu Arqueològic: Tue–Sat 10–1, 4:30–7; Sun 10–2. Museu d'Història: Tue–Sat 10–5:30; Sun 10–3
💰 Moderate (combined ticket)

MUSEU I NECROPOLIA PALEOCRISTIANS ★★
Tarragona's most treasured Roman remains are housed in the Museu i Necropolia Paleocristians (Paleo-Christian Museum), in what was once an ancient necropolis, a 20-minute walk west of the city centre. It includes a valuable collection of mosaics, pottery, metalwork, glass and ivory.

† 80B1
✉ Passeig de la Independència s/n
☎ 977 21 11 75
🕐 Tue–Sat 10–1, 4:30–7; Sun 10–2
💰 Moderate

PASSEIG ARQUEOLÒGIC ★★
For an overview of the old city and the flat hinterland of the Camp de Tarragona, walk the Passeig Arqueològic, a promenade which encircles the northernmost half of the old town, around the Roman walls, of which 1km of the original 4km remains. Seven defence towers and gates still stand, giving access to the city.

† 80B1
✉ Passeig Arqueològic
🕐 Tue–Sat, Jul–Sep 10–midnight; Oct–Mar 10–5:30; Apr–Jun 10–8, Sun 10–3
💰 Moderate

WALK

Around Tarragona's Old Town

Distance
1½ km

Time
1 hour (without visits)

Start/end point
Ajuntament, Plaça de la Font
✚ 80B1

Coffee-break
🍴 Can Peret (£)
✉ Plaça de la Font 6
☎ 977 23 76 25

An ancient well in fascinating Tarragona

Start in Plaça de la Font. Take Carrer del Cós del Bou, at the opposite end to the Ajuntament building, up to the Circ Romà.

These ruins are all that remain of Tarragona's Roman Circus, which once occupied the Plaça de la Font.

Continue up Baixada de la Peixateria, turn right into Carrer de l'Enrajolat and immediately left into Plaça del Rei.

The Museu Arqueològic and the Museu d'Història (➤ 89) provide a useful overview of the early history of Tarragona.

A small unmarked street beside the Museu Arqueològic leads to Plaça dels Angels. From here go left, then first right along Carrer Santa Anna as far as Plaça del Forum.

Of particular interest here is a section of wall and the ruins of the Roman Forum, currently under excavation.

Take Carrer Merceria past the Gothic arches, then climb the steps to the Catedral (➤ 89). Circle this magnificent building anticlockwise. In Plaça de Palau, steps lead down to Carrer Claustre and the entrance to the Cathedral and the cloister.

The medieval cloisters here, bathed in light filtered through arches and trees, provide an atmospheric retreat from the city.

Return to Plaça de Palau. Turn left down Carrer de la Guitarra, through Plaça Sant Joan, along Baixada del Roser (alongside the old city wall) and left into Plaça del Paillol. Follow the road round into Carrer dels Cavalers past Casa Castellarnau (one of Tarragona's finest medieval mansions). A right turn into Carrer Major swings round into Baixada Misericordia and brings you back to the main square, Plaça de la Font.

Where To...

Eat and Drink	92–100
Stay	101–3
Shop	104–9
Take the Children	110–11
Be Entertained	112–16

Above: *the funfair at Montjuïc*
Right: *Gaudí wall plaque at the entrance to Parc Güell*

WHERE TO EAT & DRINK

Barcelona

Prices

Restaurant prices are approximate, based on a three-course meal for one without drinks and service. All the cafés and *tapas* bars fall under the (£) category unless marked to the contrary.

£   = under 2,500 ptas
££ = 2,500 – 5,000 ptas
£££ = over 5,000 ptas

Most restaurants offer a fixed price meal (*menú del día*) of around 1,000 ptas – usually including a choice of appetiser, main course, dessert and wine – which is great value but restrictive. Eating *à la carte* is more expensive but it enables you to try some of the unusual dishes. Usually the price on the menu includes VAT (IVA). If not, it should be clearly displayed on the menu. After the meal, leave a tip of about 10 per cent of the total bill, depending on quality and service.

Restaurants

Old City

Agut d'Avignon (£££)
Hidden up an alleyway off Calle d'Avinyó at the heart of the Barri Gòtic, with classic Catalan cuisine that attracts politicians, artists, and even the King of Spain.
✉ **Calle de la Trinidad 3** ☎ **93 302 60 34** Ⓜ **Jaume I**

Amaya (££)
Popular Basque restaurant, featuring *angulas* (baby eels) and *besugo* (sea bream) and regional wines.
✉ **La Rambla 20–24** ☎ **93 302 10 37** Ⓜ **Liceu**

Barbacoa Japonesa Den (££)
Small Japanese restaurant, serving the usual *sushi*, *sashimi* and *tempura* along with the speciality, *yakiniku* – a DIY barbecue at your table.
✉ **Carrer Quintana 4** ☎ **93 302 49 69** Ⓜ **Liceu**

La Bella Napoli (£)
This lively restaurant serves the best pizzas in town.
✉ **Carrer Margarit 14** ☎ **93 442 50 46** 🕐 **Tue–Sun 1:30–4, 8–midnight** Ⓜ **Paral.lel, Poble Sec**

Biocenter (£)
The best-known of Barcelona's very few vegetarian restaurants, the Biocenter serves a range of delicious soups, casseroles and copious quantities of salad.
✉ **Carrer Pintor Fortuny 25** ☎ **93 301 45 83** 🕐 **Mon–Sat 9AM–11PM** Ⓜ **Catalunya**

Brasserie Flo (££)
Famous French-founded brasserie in a handsomely converted textile warehouse. Specialities include *foie gras* and Alsatian-style ham with *choucroute* (sauerkraut).
✉ **Carrer Jonqueres 10** ☎ **93 319 31 02** Ⓜ **Urquinaona**

Bunga Raya (££)
A Malaysian-Indonesian restaurant serving unusual vegetarian dishes and an excellent set *rijstaffel* menu.
✉ **Carrer Assaonadors 7** ☎ **93 319 31 69** 🕐 **Dinner only, Tue–Sun 8PM–1AM** Ⓜ **Jaume I**

Café de l'Academia (££)
One of Barcelona's best-value restaurants, with generous helpings of delicious Mediterranean cuisine in the heart of the old city.
✉ **Carrer Lledó 1** ☎ **93 319 82 53** 🕐 **Closed weekends** Ⓜ **Jaume I**

Can Culleretes (££)
One of the oldest restaurants in the city, founded in 1786, and traditionally decorated with wrought-iron chandeliers and signed photographs of visiting celebrities. Among the highlights of the Catalan cuisine on the menu is *perdiz* (partridge).
✉ **Carrer Quintana 5** ☎ **93 317 30 22** 🕐 **Lunch: Tue–Sun 1:30–4; dinner: Tue–Sat 9–11PM** Ⓜ **Liceu**

Ca l'Isidre (£££)
Sophisticated bistro offering exceptional Catalan cuisine and an extensive wine list. Frequented by King Juan Carlos, despite its downmarket location.
✉ **Carrer Les Flors 12** ☎ **93 441 11 39** 🕐 **Closed Sun and hols** Ⓜ **Paral.lel (best by taxi)**

WHERE TO EAT & DRINK

Los Caracoles (££)
Popular with both tourists and locals, and particularly famous for its robust, country-style cuisine, especially the spit-roasted chicken, and its namesake, snails.
✉ **Calle Escudellers 14** ☎ **93 302 31 85** Ⓜ **Drassanes, Liceu**

Casa Leopoldo (£££)
Family-run seafood restaurant, in seedy location in the Barri Xinés. Arrive by taxi! Its *tapas* bar is also hugely popular, with its barnacles, cuttlefish and baby eels.
✉ **Carrer Sant Rafael 24** ☎ **93 441 30 14** Ⓒ **Closed holiday eves and Mon** Ⓜ **Liceu**

La Cuineta (££)
Well-established restaurant in the Barri Gòtic, serving authentic dishes from northeastern Spain. Good-value fixed-price menu.
✉ **Carrer Paradis 4** ☎ **93 315 01 11** Ⓜ **Jaume 1**

Egipte (££)
Small restaurant behind the Boqueria market, serving hearty Catalan cuisine such as cod in a cream sauce or stuffed aubergine.
✉ **Carrer Jerusalem 3 & 12 (also La Rambla 79)** ☎ **93 317 74 80 or 93 301 62 08 or 93 317 95 45** Ⓒ **Closed Sun** Ⓜ **Liceu**

L'Eucaliptus (£)
A tiny tiled brasserie, offering a simple menu of *torradas* (toasted open sandwiches) and *escalivada* (traditional pepper and aubergine dish) just off La Rambla.
✉ **Carrer Bonsuccés 4** ☎ **93 302 18 24** Ⓜ **Catalunya**

La Fonda (£–££)
One of Ciutat Vella's most popular restaurants, with good, yet affordable Catalan food in stylish surroundings. Be prepared to queue.
✉ **Carrer Escudellers 10** ☎ **93 301 75 15** Ⓜ **Liceu**

Garduna (£)
Impressive seafood platters and an excellent-value *menú del día* makes this the Boqueria market's most celebrated restaurant.
✉ **Carrer Morera 17–19** ☎ **93 302 43 23** Ⓒ **Closed Sun eve** Ⓜ **Liceu**

Govinda (£)
An Indian vegetarian restaurant near La Rambla.
✉ **Plaça Vila de Madrid 4–5** ☎ **93 77 29** Ⓒ **Lunch: daily 1–4; dinner: Tue–Sat 8:30–11:45** Ⓜ **Catalunya**

El Gran Café (££)
Classic restaurant, serving French and Catalan cuisine in grand turn-of-the-century surroundings.
✉ **Carrer d'Avinyó 9** ☎ **93 318 79 86** Ⓒ **Closed Sat eve, Sun** Ⓜ **Liceu**

Hofmann (£££)
Interpretations of regional dishes by Mey Hofmann, one of Spain's most talented chefs, who also runs a world-renowned cookery school on the premises (including short courses for visitors).
✉ **Carrer Argenteria 74–78** ☎ **93 319 58 89** Ⓒ **Closed Sat, Sun and Aug** Ⓜ **Jaume I** ❓ **Phone for details of special two-day cookery courses**

Nou Celler (£)
Good service and wholesome, value-for-money Catalan cooking at this rustic *bodega* near the Picasso Museum.
✉ **Carrer de la Princesa 16** ☎ **93 310 47 73** Ⓜ **Jaume 1**

El Paraguayo (££)
Specialities from Paraguay and Argentina, including barbecued meat served on wooden boards for carnivores, and salads and pastas for vegetarians.
✉ **Carrer Parc 1** ☎ **93 302 14 41** Ⓜ **Drassanes**

Opening Times
The restaurants on these pages are all open for lunch and dinner daily unless otherwise stated. Most establishments serve lunch from around 1 to 3:30 or 4. Dinner normally starts at 8:30 or 9, and is often served until midnight or the early hours of the morning. Many cafés and *tapas* bars remain open from early morning until late at night. It is advisable to book in most restaurants, especially at weekends. Nearly all restaurants close briefly for annual holidays (dates not listed) so phone first to avoid disappointment.

Where Should We Go?
In the Old City and Gràcia, you will find small, generally reasonably priced restaurants. The Eixample is more up-market, but it also has a smattering of cheaper eateries, fast-food joints and some excellent *tapas* bars. For seafood, try La Barceloneta for traditional atmosphere or, for something more sophisticated, the Port Olímpic.

WHERE TO EAT & DRINK

Dinner in La Barceloneta
'There is an undeniable charm in the *chiringuitos* (seafood restaurants) lining the beach like dominoes at the sea's edge...and the crowds on seemingly perpetual vacation strolling to and fro...one goes to La Barceloneta as much for the ambience as the food.'
(Llorenç Torrado, local journalist)

La Perla Nera (£)
Authentic flavours, perfect pastas and an attractive dining room, brimming with fresh flowers are the trademark of this deservedly well-respected Italian restaurant.
✉ **Via Laietana 32–4** ☎ 93 310 56 46 Ⓜ Jaume I

El Pintor (££)
Traditional Catalan cuisine, fine regional wines, and a cosy, brick-vaulted interior with crisp white linen and candlelight.
✉ **Carrer St Honorat 7** ☎ 93 310 40 65 Ⓜ Jaume I

Pitarra (£)
An old-fashioned Spanish restaurant in the Barri Gòtic, named after the 19th-century Catalan playwright who lived and wrote his plays and poetry here. Don't miss the Valencian paella.
✉ **Carrer d'Avinyó 56** ☎ 93 301 16 47 🕓 Closed Sun and Aug Ⓜ Liceu

Porto Mar (££)
A Brazilian bar-restaurant where you can sample authentic Brazilian cuisine and listen to live music most weekends.
✉ **Carrer Josep Anselm Clavé 19** ☎ 93 301 82 27 Ⓜ Drassanes

Els Quatre Gats (££)
Many famous artists and intellectuals used to gather in this popular *Modernista* café in the early 1900s. Even the menu was designed by Picasso.
✉ **Carrer Montsió 3** ☎ 93 302 41 40 Ⓜ Catalunya

Les Quinze Nits (££)
Under the same management as La Fonda (➤ 93), this wood-panelled restaurant serves an exceptional, Catalan style. *civet de conill* (rabbit stew) and an impressive *parillada de peix* (seafood mixed grill).
✉ **Plaça Reial 6** ☎ 93 317 30 75 Ⓜ Liceu

Quo Vadis (£££)
One of Barcelona's finest restaurants, near the Boqueria market, serving time-tested recipes from all over Spain.
✉ **Carrer Carme 7** ☎ 93 317 74 47 🕓 Closed Sun Ⓜ Liceu

La Rioja (£–££)
This bright, white-tiled restaurant offers a splendid selection of Riojan dishes and wines, and a good-value *menú del día*.
✉ **Carrer Duran i Bas 5** ☎ 93 301 22 98 🕓 Closed Sat eve, Sun and Aug Ⓜ Catalunya

Set Portes (£££)
One of Barcelona's most historic restaurants, with waiters in long white aprons, serving excellent Catalan cuisine in traditional surroundings. It has always attracted an illustrious clientele.
✉ **Passeig de Isabel II, 14** ☎ **93 319 30 33** Ⓜ **Barceloneta**

Seafront
Agua (££)
Located right on the Barceloneta beach, near the Port Olímpic. The menu is creative, yet also offers traditional Barceloneta fare, with the emphasis on rice-based dishes.
✉ **Passeig Marítimo de la Barceloneta 30** ☎ 93 225 12 72 🕓 Closed Sun eve Ⓜ Ciutadella

El Cangrejo Loco (££)
Popular fish restaurant at the far end of the Port Olímpic but worth the walk for its extensive *pica-pica* starters and delicious main dishes – try *fideua*, cod fried in honey.
✉ **Moll de Gregal 29–30, Port Olímpic** ☎ 93 221 05 33 Ⓜ Ciutadella

WHERE TO EAT & DRINK

Can Majó (£££)
The city's top seafood restaurant, in La Barceloneta. The *suquet de peix* (mixed fish casserole), *arrozes* (black rice) with *bacalao* (salt cod) or lobster, and *centollos* (crabs from the north coast) are truly delicious.

✉ **Carrer Almirall Aixade 23** ☎ **93 221 58 18** ⓘ **Closed Sun eve and Mon** Ⓜ **Barceloneta**

La Dorada (££)
A jolly fish restaurant in the Port Olímpic, decked out like a New World-bound ocean steamer, serving the freshest of fish.

✉ **Moll de Gregal 20–21, Port Olímpic** ☎ **93 221 00 66** Ⓜ **Ciutadella**

Gambrinus (££)
This harbourside restaurant is perhaps as well known for the giant lobster sculpture on the roof as for its delectable fish dishes (➤ 74).

✉ **Moll de la Fusta 5** ☎ **93 221 96 07** ⓘ **Closed Mon–Wed** Ⓜ **Drassanes**

Llevataps (££–£££)
On the harbour's edge in the newly restored Palau de Mar (➤ 58), with outside tables. The emphasis here is on Mediterranean seafood specialities.

✉ **Palau de Mar, Plaça Pau Vila s/n** ☎ **93 221 24 27** ⓘ **Closed Sun eve** Ⓜ **Barceloneta**

El Passadís d'el Pep (£££)
There's no menu here, just some of the best fish in town. Choose from bream, bass, oysters, shellfish or the catch of the day.

✉ **Pla del Palau 2** ☎ **93 310 10 21** ⓘ **Closed Sun and hols** Ⓜ **Barceloneta**

El Petit Miau (£)
Popular, *Modernista*-inspired Catalan restaurant on the waterfront in Maremagnum (➤ 72), with beautiful stained-glass skylights, and paintings by up-and-coming local artists.

✉ **Moll d'Espanya 105 – Port Vell** ☎ **93 225 81 10** Ⓜ **Drassanes**

Planet Hollywood (£–££)
Californian cuisine in a spectacular beach setting.

✉ **Calle Marina 19–21, Marina Village** ☎ **93 221 11 11** Ⓜ **Ciutadella**

Eixample & Gràcia
Beltxenea (£££)
Barcelona's premier Basque restaurant, set in an elegant 19th-century *Modernista* building, with a pretty interior garden terrace.

✉ **Carrer Mallorca 275** ☎ **93 215 30 24** ⓘ **Closed Sat lunch, all day Sun, Aug and hols** Ⓜ **Diagonal, Passeig de Gràcia**

Botafumiero (£££)
This Galician seafood restaurant serves fish (flown in daily from Galicia) with regional wines and Catalan *cavas*. The *mariscos Botafumiera* (seafood platter) is a sight to behold.

✉ **Carrer de Gran de Gràcia 81** ☎ **93 218 42 30** ⓘ **Closed Sun eve** Ⓜ **Fontana**

El Caballito Blanco (£)
The 'Little White Horse' is a cheerful, good-value, traditional restaurant, always packed with locals.

✉ **Carrer Mallorca 196** ☎ **93 453 10 33** ⓘ **Closed Sun eve, Mon and Aug** Ⓜ **Hospital Clinic**

Casa Lorca (£)
An Andalusian restaurant in Gracia. Try gazpacho or *ajoblanco* (cold garlic soup) to start, followed by the daily catch *a la Andaluza*.

✉ **Carrer Laforja 8** ☎ **93 218 16 40** Ⓜ **Gràcia**

Tapas

The term *tapas* is thought to come from the habit of having a snack with a pre-meal drink to *tapar el apetito* ('put a lid on the appetite'). *Tapas* consist of small portions of fish, meat or vegetables, whereas *raciones* are bigger portions and usually enough for a light meal.

WHERE TO EAT & DRINK

A Sweet Tooth
Catalan desserts are often uninspiring – a choice between *gelat* (ice-cream), *flam* (crême caramel), *crèma catalana* (crème brulée), *macedonia* (fruit salad) or *formatge* (cheese). But look out for *mel i mató* (curd cheese with honey), *postre de músic* (spiced fruit cake), *panellets* (marzipans), *torrons* (nougats) and *cocas* (pastries sprinkled with sugar and pine-nuts).

Citrus (££)
Recently opened, this first-floor restaurant serves seasonal Mediterranean cuisine.
✉ Passeig de Gràcia 44
☎ 93 487 23 45

Conducta Ejemplar – Le Rodizio (££)
The speciality here is a *rodizio* – Brazilian meat buffet – with an eat-as-much-as-you-like hot and cold buffet and 12 different types of meat.
✉ Carrer Consell de Cent 403
☎ 93 265 51 12 ⏰ Lunch Mon–Sat 1–4; dinner Mon–Thu 8:30–midnight 🚇 Girona

La Dama (£££)
The French cuisine of this Michelin star-rated restaurant rivals that of the top restaurants of Paris. An added bonus is the exceptional *Modernista* setting.
✉ Avinguda Diagonal 423
☎ 93 202 06 86 🚇 Provença

Fresco (£)
Eat-as-much-as-you-want from the self-service salads, pasta, pizza, ice-cream, bread and beverages. Take-away service also available. Founded by Jordi Arrese, silver medallist in the Barcelona Olympics. Also at Ronda Universitat 29 (☎ 93 301 68 37).
✉ Carrer València 263 ☎ 93 488 10 49 🚇 Passeig de Gràcia

El Glop (£)
Crowded restaurant serving chargrilled meat and seasonal vegetables at reasonable prices, washed down with cheap Catalan wines.
✉ Carrer Sant Lluís 24 (also at Carrer Albert Llanas 2, Carrer Casp 21 and Rambla Catalunya 65) ☎ 93 213 70 58 ⏰ Closed Mon 🚇 Joanic

Jean Luc Figueras (£££)
Exquisite culinary delights served in striking surroundings of tangerine and pale-green ceramics, and enhanced by original art deco silverware.
✉ Carrer Santa Teresa 10
☎ 93 415 28 77 ⏰ Closed Sat lunch, Sun 🚇 Diagonal

Madrid-Barcelona (££)
Charming café-restaurant in a converted railway station. Dishes are served *a la brasa* – cooked on a coal-fired range.
✉ Carrer d'Aragó 282 ☎ 93 215 70 26 🚇 Passeig de Gràcia

El Racó d'en Freixa (£££)
Highly original cooking makes this one of the city's most popular Sunday-lunch haunts. Save room for the puddings which come in threes – bananas, fried, baked and caramelised, or a trio of iced, warm and hot chocolate delights.
✉ Carrer Sant Elies 22 ☎ 93 209 75 59 ⏰ Closed Mon, Sun eve & Aug 🚇 Plaça Molina/Sant Gervasi

Suburbs
La Balsa (££)
International cuisine served at the top of this circular tower, originally built as a water cistern.
✉ Carrer Infanta Isabel 4, Sant Gervasi ☎ 93 211 50 48
⏰ Closed Sun and Mon eve
🚇 Tibidabo

Bogui (£)
In the main square of the Poble Espanyol and popular with tourists, serving traditional Catalan fare. Entrance to the Poble is free if you book a table in advance.
✉ Plaza Mayor, Poble Espanyol ☎ 93 424 93 60
⏰ Closed Mon lunch
🚌 13, 61

Can Cortada (£££)
The beautiful buildings that make up one of Barcelona's most distinguished restaurants were built in the 11th

WHERE TO EAT & DRINK

century, when the Lords of Horta decided to build a defence tower in the event of possible feudal attacks.
✉ Avinguda de l'Estatut de Catalunya s/n, Horta ☎ 93 427 23 15 Ⓜ Montbau, Horta

Can Travinou (£££)
One of Barcelona's most celebrated restaurants, set in a beautiful 18th-century *masia* (farmhouse) and garden, on a hill above Horta. The wine list extends to 500 wines and *cavas*.
✉ Camí de Sant Cebrià, Horta ☎ 93 428 03 01 ⓘ Closed Sun eve Ⓜ Montbau

El Dorado Petit (£££)
This villa-restaurant, high above the city in the Sarrià district, specialises in traditional 'surf'n'turf' recipes of the Girona province, such as *pollastre amb lagostins* (chicken with lobster).
✉ Carrer Dolors Monserdà 51, Sarrià ☎ 93 204 55 06 Ⓜ Reina Elisenda, Sarrià

Gaig (£££)
A famous family-run restaurant, founded in 1869 as a café for cart drivers. It is now one of Barcelona's most upmarket eateries.
✉ Passeig Maragall 402 ☎ 93 429 10 17 ⓘ Closed Sun and Mon hols (eve) and Aug Ⓜ Vilapicina

Neichel (£££)
This stylish restaurant boasts Alsace-born chef Jean-Louis Neichel, who has been described as 'the most brilliant ambassador French cuisine has ever had within Spain'.
✉ Avinguda Pedralbes 16 bis ☎ 93 203 84 08 ⓘ Closed Sat lunch, Sun, Aug and hols Ⓜ Palau Reial

Les Noies (££)
Characterful old restaurant serving unusual Catalan dishes, often combining sweet and savoury flavours, such as partridge with grapes or duck stuffed with figs.
✉ Carrer Major de Sarrià 109, Sarrià ☎ 93 205 09 59 Ⓜ Reina Elisenda, Sarrià

La Parra (£-££)
Country cooking in an old coaching inn with hearty portions of lamb, rabbit, steak and spare ribs cooked on a giant wood-fired grill, and served on wooden slabs with lashings of homemade *allioli* (➤ 52).
✉ Carrer Joanot Martorell 3, Hostafranca ☎ 93 332 51 34 ⓘ Closed Mon–Fri lunch Ⓜ Hostafranca

La Venta (££)
The conservatory and terrace, combined with a light, imaginative menu, is perfect for spring lunches or summer nights.
✉ Plaça Dr Andreu, Sant Gervasi ☎ 93 212 64 55 ⓘ Closed Sun Ⓜ Avinguda Tibidabo then Tramvia Blau

Cafés and Tapas Bars

Old City
Ambos Mundos
Pleasant *cerveceria* (beer bar) in Plaça Reial serving wholesome tapas in terracotta dishes.
✉ Plaça Reial ☎ 93 317 01 66 ⓘ Closed Tue Ⓜ Liceu

Bar del Pi
Hugely popular, despite its small *tapas* selection, in one of Barcelona's most atmospheric squares.
✉ Plaça Sant Josep Oriol 1 ☎ 93 302 21 23 Ⓜ Liceu

El Bosc de les Fades
An extraordinary café-cum-magic fairy world, decorated with fountains, toadstools and fairytale princesses.
✉ Passatge de la Banca, La Rambla 4–6 ☎ 93 317 26 49 Ⓜ Drassanes

'Cafè Sol, Per Favor'
Start the day with a *cafè amb llet* (a large milky coffee). After mid-morning, drink a *tallat* (a small coffee with a dash of milk), a *cafè sol* (espresso) or a *cafè americano*. *Descafeinado* is widely available but order it *de máquina* (espresso-style). After dinner, why not try a *carajillo* (a *sol* with a shot of brandy)?

WHERE TO EAT & DRINK

Bodegas, Cervecerias and Orxaterias

There are bars on every second street in Barcelona – cosy, old-fashioned *bodegas*, serving wine from the barrel, and *cervecerias* or beer bars, offering both local beer on draught (*una cana*) and pricier imported beers. Or visit an *orxateria* and try *orxata*, the refreshing, milk-like drink made from crushed *chufa* nuts, and unique to Spain.

Café del Museu Picasso
Photos of Picasso line the walls of this smart café, and the salads are named after his paintings.
✉ **Carrer Montcada 15–17**
☎ **93 268 30 21** 🚇 **Jaume I**
❓ **No need to pay museum entrance**

Cafè de l'Opera
This original 19th-century café is one of Barcelona's favourites, and the best terrace-café along the Ramblas.
✉ **La Rambla 74** ☎ **93 317 75 85** 🚇 **Liceu**

Celta
A Galician bar near the port, known for its fried *rabas* (squid) and its *patatas bravas*, (potatoes in a spicy mayonnaise), serving Galician white wine in traditional white ceramic cups.
✉ **Carrer Mercè 16** ☎ **93 315 00 06** 🕐 **Mon–Sat 10AM–1AM; Sun 10AM–midnight**
🚇 **Drassanes**

Dulcinea
The most famous chocolate shop in town. Try *melindros* (sugar-topped sponge fingers) dipped in very thick hot chocolate.
✉ **Via Petritxol 21** ☎ **93 302 68 24** 🚇 **Liceu**

Forn de Betlem
A bright orange, trendy café and cake shop near the Museum of Contemporary Art (▶ 50), one of very few places around the museum for a coffee or a snack.
✉ **Carrer Joaquín Costa 24**
☎ **93 412 42 17** 🚇 **Universitat**

Hard Rock Café
The latest addition to the world-famous chain.
✉ **Plaça Catalunya 21** ☎ **93 270 23 05** 🚇 **Catalunya**

Hivernacle
Elegant café inside the Parc de la Ciutadella's beautiful 19th-century greenhouse. Occasional live jazz or classical music.
✉ **Parc de la Ciutadella**
☎ **93 268 01 77** 🚇 **Arc de Triomf**

Mesón del Café
Join locals at the bar for a coffee or hot chocolate here while exploring the Barri Gòtic.
✉ **Calle de la Librateria 16**
☎ **93 315 07 54** 🚇 **Jaume I**

Naviera
Although the concept of *tapas* on La Rambla sounds dear, this is surprisingly good value.
✉ **La Rambla de Canaletas 127**
☎ **93 301 92 25** 🚇 **Catalunya**

La Plata
One of several *tascas* (traditional bars) on this narrow medieval street, specialising in whitebait, anchovies, and tomato and onion salads.
✉ **Carrer Mercè 28** ☎ **93 315 10 09** 🚇 **Drassanes**

Tèxtil Cafè
Delicious quiches and salads, in the courtyard of the medieval palace which houses the Museu Tèxtil.
✉ **Carrer Montcada 12** ☎ **93 268 25 98** 🚇 **Jaume I** ❓ **No need to pay museum entrance**

La Vinya del Senyor
A modern, stand-up wine bar beside Santa Maria del Mar.
✉ **Plaça Santa Maria 5** ☎ **93 310 33 79** 🚇 **Jaume I**

Seafront
Can Ramonet
This is a stand-up *tapas* bar in one of La Barceloneta's top fish restaurants. It is worth trying their mussels, 'from the beach'.
✉ **Carrer Maquinista 17**
☎ **93 319 30 64**
🚇 **Barceloneta**

WHERE TO EAT & DRINK

Goyescas
An eye-popping choice of *tapas* on the first floor of the Hotel Arts, overlooking the Port Olímpic.
✉ Hotel Arts, Carrer de la Manna 19 ☎ 93 221 10 00
🚇 Ciutadella

Rey de la Gamba
The 'King of Prawns' serves seafood and cured hams, and is especially busy at weekends.
✉ Passeig Joan de Borbó 53 (also Moll Mistral, Port Olímpic)
☎ 93 221 75 98
🚇 Barceloneta

El Vaso del Oro
One of very few *cervecerias* (beer bars) that brews its own beers.
✉ Carrer Balboa 6 ☎ 93 319 30 98 🚇 Barceloneta

Eixample & Gràcia
Ba-Ba-Reeba
The *tapas* selection here includes prawns wrapped in bacon, stuffed mussels and sea urchins filled with melted cheese.
✉ Passeig de Gràcia 28
☎ 93 301 43 02 🚇 Passeig de Gràcia

Bodega Sepúlveda
Boquerones (fresh anchovies) are the speciality at this genuine locals' bar.
✉ Carrer Sepúlveda 173 bis
☎ 93 323 59 44 🚇 Universitat

La Bodegueta
An old wine tavern, well known for its Catalan *charcuterie*, accompanied by a wide selection of local wines and vermouths.
✉ Rambla de Catalunya 100
☎ 93 215 48 94 🚇 Passeig de Gràcia, Provença

Ciudat Condal Cerveceria
A popular meeting-place in the centre of town for breakfast or coffee.
✉ Rambla de Catalunya 18
☎ 93 318 19 97 🚇 Catalunya

Fashion Café
The first 'Fashion Café' outside America, opened by supermodels Naomi Campbell and Claudia Schiffer, stages fashion shows every Tuesday, Wednesday and Thursday at 10PM.
✉ Paseo de Gràcia 56 ☎ 93 215 49 99 🚇 Passeig de Gràcia

Flash-Flash Tortilleria (£)
Cheap, healthy Spanish fast food – *tortillas* (omelettes) and salad.
✉ Carrer Granada del Penedes 25 ☎ 93 237 09 90
🚇 Diagonal

Pla de la Garsa
A former 16th-century stables and dairy near the Picasso Museum, now a beautiful bar-restaurant, known for its cheeses, pâtés and hams.
✉ Carrer Assaonadors 13
☎ 93 315 24 13 🚇 Jaume I

Qu-Qu (Quasi Queviures)
A delicatessen-cum-*tapas* bar, specialising in salads, cheeses and Catalan sausage meats.
✉ Passeig de Gràcia 24
☎ 93 317 45 12 🚇 Passeig de Gràcia

Tapa Tapa
This *cerveceria* is the in-place in town to meet for *tapas* and a beer. Specials include snails, fried pig snout, black squid and octopus.
✉ Passeig de Gràcia 44
☎ 93 488 33 69 🚇 Passeig de Gràcia

Valentin
This *xarcuteria* specialises solely in cold cuts. Try *raciones* of their delicious *chorizo*, *salchichón* and *Bellota* ham or a mixed platter of cold cuts.
✉ Carrer Diputación 301
☎ 93 487 23 72 🚇 Passeig de Gràcia

Regional Cuisine
Barcelona boasts restaurants to suit all tastes, budgets and occasions. Contrary to what many visitors assume, there is no such thing as 'Spanish national cuisine' but rather a wide variety of regional styles, such as Galician, Basque, Castilian and Andalusian, all to be found in Barcelona.

WHERE TO EAT & DRINK

Catalonia

Pa amb Tomàquet
No Catalan meal is complete without *pa amb tomàquet* – a hearty slice (*llesque*) of white country bread rubbed with a ripe tomato, with a drizzle of olive oil and a pinch of salt. There are even restaurants called *llesqueria*, which specialise solely in '*pa-amb-t*' with a variety of toppings.

Restaurants and Cafés/Bars

Girona
L'Arcada (£)
Chic café bar-cum-restaurant underneath Rambla Llibertat's handsome arcade.
✉ **Rambla Llibertat 38** ☎ **972 20 10 15**

Cipresaia (££)
Smart, sophisticated restaurant, at the heart of the old Jewish quarter.
✉ **Carrer General Fornas 2** ☎ **972 21 14 83**

El Pou de Call (££)
Local cuisine in traditional surroundings. Excellent-value *menú del diá* and wine list.
✉ **Carrer de la Força 14** ☎ **972 22 37 74**

Montserrat
Abat Cisneros (££)
Montserrat's top restaurant. The 16th-century stone dining-room used to contain the monastery stables.
✉ **Hotel Abat Cisneros** ☎ **93 835 02 01**

Sitges
Chiringuito (£)
A traditional-style *tapas* bar in a small wooden hut on the seafront, specialising in fresh sardines, salads and sandwiches. Sunny terrace.
✉ **Passeig de la Ribera** ☎ **93 894 75 96**

Mare Nostrum (££)
Sophisticated waterfront restaurant. Start with the *Xato de Sitges* (grilled fish with a local variant of *romesco* sauce, ► 53), followed by monkfish and prawns with garlic mousseline.
✉ **Passeig de la Ribera 60–62** ☎ **93 894 33 93**

Tarragona
L'Ancora (£)
Delicious fishy *tapas* dishes in the bar of this characterful restaurant, decked out like the interior of a ship.
✉ **Carrer Trafalgar 25** ☎ **977 24 28 06**

Bodega Celler Gras (£)
Join the locals for *tapas* specialities – pâtés, cheeses and *charcuterie*, including spicy *xoriço* and Mallorquin *sobrassada*.
✉ **Carrer Governadir Gonzalez 8** ☎ **977 23 48 20**

Can Llesques (£)
A small, rustic restaurant with low stone arches in the old town, with wine served in ceramic pitchers.
✉ **Carrer Natzaret 6, Plaça del Rei**

Sol-Ric (££)
This top fish restaurant is located on the outskirts of town near Platja Rembassada.
✉ **Via Augusta 227** ☎ **977 23 20 32**

Vilafranca del Penedès
Bar Tanit (£)
This is a cheerful, locals' bar, with a traditional, tiled interior and good *tapas*. The *menú del diá* represents reasonable value.
✉ **Carrer del Casal 1** ☎ **93 817 09 97**

Cal Ton (££)
It may come as a surprise to find such a smart, modern restaurant in an otherwise traditional town. Try their pancakes filled with a seafood and *cava* sauce.
✉ **Carrer del Casal 8** ☎ **93 890 37 41**

WHERE TO STAY

Barcelona

Arts (£££)
Barcelona's most fashionable hotel provides state-of-the-art, unabashed luxury beside the sea (▶ panel).
✉ **Carrer de la Marina 19–21**
☎ **93 221 10 00**
🚇 **Ciutadella/Vila Olímpica**

Barcelona Hilton (£££)
High-amenity hotel, 15 minutes from the airport, at the heart of the city's commercial and financial district. Ideal for both business and leisure travellers.
✉ **Avinguda Diagonal 589–591**
☎ **93 495 77 77** 🚇 **Maria Cristina**

Citadines (££)
A 3-star 'aparthotel' on the Ramblas, with a rooftop terrace overlooking part of the Old City (▶ 102).
✉ **La Rambla 122** ☎ **93 270 11 11** 🚇 **Catalunya/Liceu**

Claris (£££)
Situated just off the exclusive Passeig de Gràcia, this impressive deluxe hotel features modern accommodation furnished in marble, glass and works of art. Facilities include several restaurants, a roof terrace with pool, a fitness centre, a Japanese garden and even a museum of priceless Egyptian antiques.
✉ **Carrer Pau Claris 150**
☎ **93 487 62 62** 🚇 **Passeig de Gràcia**

Colón (££–£££)
This old-fashioned, family-friendly hotel, opposite the cathedral, has more of a country-home atmosphere than that of a busy city hotel.
✉ **Avenida de la Catedral 7**
☎ **93 301 14 04** 🚇 **Jaume I/Urquinaona**

Condes De Barcelona (£££)
A stylish hotel in Barcelona's main shopping district, with elegant public rooms, and bedrooms furnished in *Modernista* style.
✉ **Passeig de Gràcia 73–75**
☎ **93 488 22 00** 🚇 **Diagonal**

Duques De Bergara (££)
This attractive 4-star hotel offers contemporary elegance in a turn-of-the-century building.
✉ **Carrer Bergara 11** ☎ **93 301 51 51** 🚇 **Catalunya**

Gallery (£££)
You are guaranteed a warm welcome and a relaxing stay at this lovely, central hotel. Ask for their leaflet detailing five city strolls.
✉ **Carrer Roselló 249** ☎ **93 415 99 11** 🚇 **Diagonal**

Gaudí (£)
Facing Palau Güell, one of Gaudí's masterworks, this modern 3-star hotel has 73 well-equipped rooms and a Gaudí-inspired reception area.
✉ **Carrer Nou de la Rambla 12**
☎ **93 317 90 32**
🚇 **Drassanes/Liceu**

Gran Hotel Barcino (££)
Modern luxury and tastefully furnished rooms await you at the Barcino, the heart of the Barri Gòtic.
✉ **Carrer Jaume I, 6** ☎ **93 302 20 12** 🚇 **Jaume I**

Granvía (£)
It is easy to imagine how splendid this reasonably priced hotel must have been in its heyday with its old-world gilt, balustraded staircase and chandeliers.
✉ **Gran Via de les Cortes Catalanes 642** ☎ **93 318 19 00**
🚇 **Catalunya**

Prices
Prices are based on the cost of a double room per night (excluding breakfast and tax).

£££ over 25,000 ptas
££ 15,000-25,000 ptas
£   under 15,000 ptas

Symbol of Perfection
Hotel Arts, the highest building in Spain and Barcelona's only waterfront hotel, towers above the entrance to the Port Olímpic. Its post-Modern interior is filled with modern Catalan art and on its waterfront terraces, a vast copper fish designed by Frank Gehry (▶ 74) has become a new symbol of the city.

WHERE TO STAY

Hotel Construction
Several new hotels have been constructed at the top of La Rambla, in an attempt to revitalise this famous street. The apartment-style Citadines, designed by Esteve Bonnell, is one of the more attractive (➤ 101).

Gravina (££)
This charming 3-star hotel has a prime location, in a side street near the bustling Plaça de Catalunya, and has recently been totally refurbished.

✉ **Carrer Gravina 12** ☎ **93 301 68 68** Ⓜ **Universitat**

Husa Palace (£££)
Part of the 'Leading Hotels in the World' group, this is a gracious hotel with old-world charm, solicitous staff and a reputation for excellent cuisine and service.

✉ **Gran Via de les Corts Catalanes 668** ☎ **93 318 52 00** Ⓜ **Passeig de Gràcia**

Jardí (£)
A small, friendly hotel with clean, simple rooms overlooking two of the Barri Gòtic's prettiest squares, Plaça Sant Josep Oriol and Plaça del Pi.

✉ **Plaça Sant Josep Oriol 1** ☎ **93 301 59 00** Ⓜ **Liceu**

Méson Castilla (£)
A quiet, characterful family-run hotel on the edge of the old town, with 56 rooms furnished in traditional Castilian style.

✉ **Carrer Valldonzella 5** ☎ **93 318 21 82** Ⓜ **Universitat**

Oriente (££)
The Oriente was once *the* place to stay in Barcelona, attracting illustrious travellers such as Hans Christian Andersen, Mary Pickford, Toscanini and Errol Flynn to name a few. Recently restored but still traditionally furnished, it now draws customers seeking a taste of history.

✉ **La Rambla 45** ☎ **93 302 25 58** Ⓜ **Liceu**

Rey Juan Carlos I Conrad International (£££)
A member of the 'Leading Hotels of the World' group, set in private gardens and with extensive views of the city. First-rate facilities include indoor and outdoor pools and a health club.

✉ **Avinguda Diagonal 661–671** ☎ **93 448 08 08** Ⓜ **Zona Universitària**

Rialto (£)
The cosy atmosphere and bedrooms stylishly furnished with Catalan flair make this 3-star hotel in the Barri Gòtic an excellent choice.

✉ **Carrer Ferran 42** ☎ **93 318 52 12** Ⓜ **Jaume I**

Rivoli Ramblas (£££)
Although this fine hotel only opened in 1989, it immediately established itself as one of the best. Behind the dignified *Modernista* façade, the interior contains murals, art deco furnishings and many antiques. A rooftop terrace overlooks the smarter end of La Rambla.

✉ **La Rambla 128** ☎ **93 302 66 43** Ⓜ **Catalunya**

Roma Reial (£)
Excellent, cheap accommodation overlooking the Plaça Reial. Service is friendly and all rooms have bathroom and phone.

✉ **Plaça Reial 11** ☎ **93 302 03 66** Ⓜ **Liceu**

Sant Agustí (£)
Just off La Rambla, and near the Boqueria market, this smart, modern 3-star hotel offers excellent value in a quiet yet central location.

✉ **Plaça Sant Agustí 3** ☎ **93 318 16 58** Ⓜ **Liceu**

WHERE TO STAY

Catalonia

Figueres

Ampurdan (££)
This sylish hotel, just north of Figueres, was the birthplace of the new Catalan cuisine and is still a place of pilgrimage for food-lovers.
✉ **Antiga Carrertera de França**
☎ **972 50 05 62**

Hotel Durán (££)
This popular hotel also has a highly regarded restaurant, that serves hearty traditional cuisine with a modern touch and was a favourite lunchtime haunt of Salvador Dalí and friends.
✉ **Carrer Lasuaca 5** ☎ **972 50 12 50**

Girona

Bellmirall (£)
This characterful hotel, housed inside the ancient buildings of the Jewish quarter and near to the cathedral, feels more like a country dwelling.
✉ **Carrer Bellmirall 3** ☎ **972 20 40 09**

Carlemany (£££)
A smart, modern hotel, well placed between the station and the old town, and brimful of modern art. What's more, its restaurant is one of the best in town.
✉ **Plaça Miquel Santaló**
☎ **972 21 12 12**

Montserrat

Abat Cisneros (££)
The name of this 3-star hotel, set in Montserrat's main square, is derived from a title given to the head of Benedictine monasteries during the Middle Ages. It has cheap, basic rooms in the former monks' cells.
✉ **Plaça de Monestir, 08199 Montserrat** ☎ **93 835 02 01**

Sitges

Capri-Veracruz (£–££)
Excellent value just off the seafront, this family-run hotel consists of two houses which between them sandwich a small garden with an outdoor pool, jacuzzi and terrace.
✉ **Avinguda Sofia 13–15**
☎ **93 811 02 67**

Celimar (£–££)
A recently renovated 3-star *Modernista* hotel, with 26 rooms just a stone's throw from the beach. Ask for one with a balcony.
✉ **Passeig de Ribera 18** ☎ **93 811 0170**

El Xalet (£)
A discreet hotel in a beautiful *Modernista* villa, with just 10 well-furnished rooms, restaurant, pool and garden.
✉ **Carrer Isla de Cuba 35**
☎ **93 811 0070**

Tarragona

Fòrum (£)
Simple, clean rooms overlooking Plaça de la Font in the Old Town, above a jolly *bodega*-style restaurant.
✉ **Plaça de la Font 37** ☎ **977 23 17 18**

Imperial Tarraco (££)
Tarragona's top hotel (4-star), centrally situated and overlooking both the sea and the Amfiteatre Romà (➤ 88).
✉ **Passeig de Palmeres**
☎ **977 23 30 40**

Urbis (£)
Reasonably priced, friendly 3-star hotel in the town centre, just off the Rambla Nova and near the daily fruit market.
✉ **Carrer Reding 20 bis**
☎ **977 24 01 16**

Hotel Choices
It is advisable to make reservations in advance throughout Catalonia, especially in the cities and the coastal regions. Two types of accommodation are available – hotels (H) and pensions (P). Hotels are classified from 1- to 5-star, while pensions have 1 or 2 stars. As hotel standards vary considerably, view the room before committing yourself.

WHERE TO SHOP

Clothes, Jewellery & Accessories

Department Stores and Malls

El Corte Inglés is the city's foremost department store, with three different locations (Plaça Catalunya, Plaça Francesc Macià and Plaça Maria Cristina), and particularly strong fashion sections for men, women and children. Fashion malls include La Avenida, a small arcade of luxury shops (✉ Rambla de Catalunya 121), and Bulevard Rosa (✉ Passeig de Gràcia 55). Look out for mega-malls, Barcelona Glóries and L'Illa (✉ Diagonal 280 and 545-557) and Maremagnum.

Adolfo Domínguez

One of Spain's most famous designers, Adolfo Domínguez is renowned for introducing linen suits in the 1980s with the slogan 'wrinkles are fashionable'. He also designed this shop in the Passeig de Gràcia.
✉ **Passeig de Gràcia 89**
☎ **93 487 41 70** 🚇 **Passeig de Gràcia**

Antonio Miró

Antonio Miró is Spain's brightest young fashion star. Although best known for his men's fashions, he also designs women's and children's clothes, shoes, spectacles and furniture.
✉ **Carrer Consell de Cent 349–351** ☎ **93 487 06 70**
🚇 **Passeig de Gràcia**

Bagués

Run by an old family of gold and silversmiths, this exquisite shop on the ground floor of Casa Amatller (▶ 36) contains priceless works by Masriera, the sole creator of the *Modernista* style in the Spanish jewellery trade.
✉ **Passeig de Gràcia 41**
☎ **93 216 01 74** 🚇 **Passeig de Gràcia**

Bóboli

A leading Spanish brand for children and teens clothing. Comfortable, stylish and sporty.
✉ **Carrer Marià Cubí 1** ☎ **93 237 56 70** 🚇 **Gràcia**

Corbata Barcelona

An astonishing range of ties are on sale in this tiny shop at Port Vell.
✉ **Moll d'Espanya s/n, Maremagnum** ☎ **93 225 81 32**
🚇 **Barceloneta, Drassanes**

Cristina Castaner

All the latest trends in women's footwear, plus handbags and other accessories.
✉ **Carrer Mestre Nicolau 23**
☎ **93 414 24 28** 🚇 **Muntaner**

Gemmòleg Villegas

Striking silver costume jewellery inspired by the works of Picasso, Miró and Dalí.
✉ **Carrer Comtal 18** ☎ **93 318 60 94** 🚇 **Catalunya**

Hipòtesi

Specialising in contemporary jewellery, with regular displays of highly experimental pieces by up-and-coming designers.
✉ **237 Carrer de Provença**
☎ **93 215 02 98** 🚇 **Provença**

Joaquín Berao

Jewellery by Joaquín Berao, celebrated for his unusual combinations of materials and avant-garde chunky designs.
✉ **Rosselló 277** ☎ **93 217 70 32** 🚇 **Provença, Diagonal**

Lydia Delgado

Delgado is one of Barcelona's most distinctive local designers of easy-to-wear women's fashions. Her collections are sold in this shop alone.
✉ **Carrer Minerva 21** ☎ **93 415 99 98** 🚇 **Gràcia**

Loewe

One of the most celebrated leather-goods companies in the world, located in Domènech i Montaner's *Modernista* Lleó-Morera building.
✉ **Passeig de Gràcia 35**
☎ **93 216 04 00** 🚇 **Passeig de Gràcia**

WHERE TO SHOP

Mango
This chainstore brims with cheap, trendy designs for the truly fashionable.
✉ **Avinguda Portal de l'Àngel**
☎ **93 317 69 85** Ⓜ **Catalunya**

La Manual Alpargatera
This shop has been making traditional Spanish espadrilles with esparto soles by hand since 1910. Their footwear has been worn by such celebrities as Michael Douglas, Jack Nicholson and the Pope.
✉ **Carrer Avinyó 7** ☎ **93 301 01 72** Ⓜ **Jaume I**

Mokuba
A specialist shop with rows and rows of ribbons and braids. Every haberdasher's dream!
✉ **Carrer Consell de Cent 329**
☎ **93 488 12 77** Ⓜ **Universitat**

Muxart
This is a vibrant shop showcasing shoes by Barcelonan shoe designer, Muxart.
✉ **Carrer Roselló 230** ☎ **93 488 10 64** Ⓜ **Provença, Diagonal**

Noel Barcelona
You'll find all the latest trends in footwear here, from ankle boots to platform trainers.
✉ **Pelai 46** ☎ **93 317 86 38** Ⓜ **Catalunya**

Pedro Alonso
This small shop with its gloves, fans and imitation jewellery, once catered mainly for stage performers, but today has a more diverse clientele.
✉ **Carrer Santa Anna 27**
☎ **93 317 60 85** Ⓜ **Catalunya**

La Perla Gris
Lingerie, swimwear and corsetry by all the best Spanish and international brands.
✉ **Rambla Catalunya 112**
☎ **93 218 07 96** Ⓜ **Diagonal, Provença**

Regia
This is Barcelona's prime perfumery and it even has its own small 'Perfume Museum' at the back of the shop, which may be visited by appointment.
✉ **Passeig de Gràcia 39**
☎ **93 216 01 21** Ⓜ **Passeig de Gràcia**

Starlight
Shop here for way-out second-hand fashion, including a dazzling array of 1960s and 70s flower-power clothing.
✉ **Calle Aribau 24** ☎ **93 454 35 36** Ⓜ **Universitat**

T-40
For shoes by local designer Pilar Martin Gordillo in a tiny shop on the fringe of the Bulevard Rosa (▶ 104, panel).
✉ **Rambla Catalunya 68**
☎ **93 487 09 49** Ⓜ **Passeig de Gràcia**

Tony Mora
Floor-to-ceiling shelves of boots, including typical Spanish *campera* cowboy boots.
✉ **Passeig de Gràcia 33**
☎ **93 487 65 64** Ⓜ **Passeig de Gràcia**

Zara
A nationwide chain of trendy fashion stores, popular with young shoppers.
✉ **Carrer Pelai 58** ☎ **93 301 09 78** Ⓜ **Catalunya**

Streetwise
Barcelona has two main shopping areas. The Ciutat Vella contains many traditional shops as well as more off-beat boutiques. Try Carrer Banys Nous for arts and antique shops; Carrer Petritxol for home accessories and gift ideas; Carrer Portaferrissa and Carrer Portal de l'Angel for fashion and shoes. The Eixample's three main streets – Passeig de Gràcia, Rambla de Catalunya and the Diagonal – are a showcase for the latest in fashion and design.

WHERE TO SHOP

Art, Crafts, Gifts & Design

Museum Shops
Barcelona's museum shops stock a high-quality selection of goods such as designer items, gifts and arty souvenirs. Fundació Miró or Museu Picasso both offer a large array of fine products devoted to these artists; La Pedrera shows *Modernista* jewellery and other Gaudí-inspired gifts; and MACBA is one of the main outlets for the quality 'Made in Barcelona' range of gifts and souvenirs.

Aspectos
Design gallery featuring novelty furniture and household ornaments from established and up-and-coming Spanish designers.
✉ **Carrer Rec 28** ☎ **933 19 52 85** Ⓜ **Jaume I**

BD Ediciones de Diseno
Winner of several awards for its state-of-the-art furniture and household design, beautifully displayed in a striking *Modernista* house by Domènech i Montaner.
✉ **Carrer Mallorca 291** ☎ **93 458 69 09** Ⓜ **Diagonal**

Cereria Subirà
The oldest shop in Barcelona, founded in 1761, selling candles both ancient and modern, and religious and profane.
✉ **Baixada Llibreteria 7** ☎ **93 315 26 06** Ⓜ **Jaume I**

Coses de Casa
Handmade patchwork quilts and fabrics, including the distinctive Mallorcan *roba de llengües* (literally 'cloth of tongues'), striking for its red, blue or green zigzag patterns.
✉ **Carrer Montcada 19** ☎ **93 301 33 11** Ⓜ **Jaume I**

Galeria Surrealista
T-shirts, graphic work and other gift ideas, taking their inspiration from the work of Dalí and other Surrealists.
✉ **Carrer Montcada 19** ☎ **93 302 33 11** Ⓜ **Jaume I**

Germanes Garcia
Wickerwork of all shapes and sizes tumbles out of this village-style shop into the streets of the Old City.
✉ **Carrer Banys Nous 15** ☎ **93 318 66 46** Ⓜ **Liceu**

Ici et La
An exotic shop stocking furniture and home accessories by young Spanish designers.
✉ **Plaça Santa Maria del Mar 2** ☎ **93 216 03 46** Ⓜ **Diagonal**

D Barcelona
A wide choice of gifts and avant-garde household items, together with temporary exhibitions presenting the work of young designers alongside established names.
✉ **Avinguda Diagonal 76** ☎ **93 216 03 46** Ⓜ **Diagonal**

Dos I Una
The first design shop in Barcelona – a tiny treasure trove of gadgets and unusual gift ideas.
✉ **Carrer Rosselló 275** ☎ **93 217 70 32** Ⓜ **Diagonal**

Dou Deu
For the latest in Catalan design you shouldn't miss this unique gallery, featuring illustrations by Mariscal, desk sets by Antonio Miró, ceramics by Carlos Pazos, and other designer pieces.
✉ **Carrer Doctor Dou 10** ☎ **93 301 29 40** Ⓜ **Liceu, Catalunya**

Insolit
You won't find these decorations, furniture and gift ideas anywhere else as the owners of this distinctive shop are also the designers.
✉ **Avinguda Diagonal 353** ☎ **93 207 49 19** Ⓜ **Verdaguer**

Itaca
Folk pottery and crafted glassware from all parts of Spain, Mexico and Morocco.
✉ **Carrer Ferran 26** ☎ **93 301 30 44** Ⓜ **Liceu**

WHERE TO SHOP

Libreria Maeght
Come to these specialists in 20th-century art, design and photography for posters, prints and other graphic works. Upstairs is a prestigious art gallery.
✉ **Carrer Montcada 25** ☎ **93 301 01 72** Ⓜ **Liceu, Jaume I**

La Manual Alpargatera
All kinds of handmade, straw woven items, including hats, bags and their speciality, espadrilles.
✉ **Carrer Avinyá 7** ☎ **93 301 01 72** Ⓜ **Liceu, Jaume I**

Miniarquitectura
The miniature, handmade and hand-painted, pottery reproductions of Barcelonan buildings sold here make unusual but very distinctive souvenirs.
✉ **Carrer Boters 8** ☎ **93 412 27 07** Ⓜ **Jaume I**

Museu Picasso
One of Barcelona's many notable museum shops reflecting the city's connections with this major 20th century artist (➤ 106, panel).
✉ **Carrer Montcada 15** ☎ **93 319 63 10** Ⓜ **Jaume I**

Paragus
An old fashioned and unmistakably Spanish store, specialising in umbrellas, lace parasols, fans and silver-capped walking-sticks.
✉ **La Rambla 104** ☎ **93 301 33 26** Ⓜ **Catalunya, Liceu**

Pilma
This is an expensive store specialising in top-name furniture, textiles, household items and accessories.
✉ **Avinguda Diagonal 403** ☎ **93 416 13 99** Ⓜ **Diagonal**

Poble Espanyol
Over 60 art and craft shops in a reproduction 'Spanish Village' (➤ 22) selling traditional wares from all corners of Spain (➤ panel).
✉ **Carrer Marques de Comillas s/n** ☎ **93 325 78 66** 🚌 **13, 61**

Popul-Art
Papier mâché and ceramic sculptures in an unusual shop, opened in the 1960s by a group of young artists keen to revive traditional art methods and materials.
✉ **Carrer Montcada 22** ☎ **93 310 78 49** Ⓜ **Jaume I**

Puzzlemanía
Over a thousand different jigsaw puzzles for the amusement of young and old.
✉ **Carrer Diputació 225** ☎ **93 451 58 03** Ⓜ **Universitat**

El Rei de la Màgica
Stepping inside this extraordinary magic shop, founded in 1881, is like entering another world. An experience not to be missed!
✉ **Carrer la Princessa 11** ☎ **93 319 73 93** Ⓜ **Jaume I**

Sala Parés
Barcelona's finest gallery – specialist in 19th- and 20th-century paintings, drawings and sculptures.
✉ **Carrer Pextritxol 5** ☎ **93 318 70 20** Ⓜ **Catalunya**

Vinçon
Everything for the home. This large design 'department store' is Barcelona's answer to Terance Conran, with trendy yet practical household articles at accessible prices. In 1995 it won the National Design Prize.
✉ **Passeig de Gràcia 96** ☎ **93 215 60 50** Ⓜ **Passeig de Gràcia**

Poble Espanyol
This purpose-built 'Spanish Village' (➤ 22), with its methodically numbered shops and studios demonstrating local craft-making skills, offers a comprehensive range of Spanish and Mallorcan souvenirs. On sale are fine glassware, wood-carvings, Lladro porcelain, decorative goldware and jewellery together with flamenco costumes, guitars, fans and castanets.

WHERE TO SHOP

Antiques, Books & Music

Local Alternative to St Valentine's Day
To celebrate the day of Sant Jordi (St George), Catalonia's patron saint, couples express their love by exchanging gifts: roses for the woman and a book for the man. The Ramblas are lined with temporary bookstalls, and half of Catalonia's annual book sales take place on this day.

Angel Batlle
Antiquarian books, old maps, prints and nautical charts are in abundance here.
✉ **Carrer Palla 23** ☎ **93 301 58 84** Ⓜ **Liceu**

L'Arca de l'Avia
An Aladdin's cave of antique cottons, linens, silks. Beautiful, albeit pricey, patchwork eiderdowns and beaded bags.
✉ **Carrer Banys Nous 20** ☎ **93 302 15 98** Ⓜ **Liceu**

Artur Ramon Anticuario
Two adjacent premises displaying a wide array of antique paintings, sculpture and decorative arts.
✉ **Carrer de la Palla 25** ☎ **93 302 59 70** Ⓜ **Jaume I**

Born Subastas
This auction house holds sales every other week, but is always an interesting place in which to browse.
✉ **Carrer Bonaire 5** ☎ **93 268 34 55** Ⓜ **Jaume I, Barceloneta**

Bulevard dels Antiquaris
A spacious mall containing over 70 shops for art-lovers and antique collectors. Among the highlights, don't miss Govary's (☎ 93 215 48 92), with its porcelain doll collection, or Turn of the Century (☎ 93 215 94 62) for decorative *Modernista* pieces.
✉ **Passeig de Gràcia 55** ☎ **93 215 44 99** Ⓜ **Passeig de Gràcia**

Casa Beethoven
Founded in 1915, this shop carries scores and sheet music especially by Spanish and Catalan composers.
✉ **La Rambla 97** ☎ **93 301 48 26** Ⓜ **Liceu**

Castelló
A chain of record shops. Carrer Tallers 3 has one of the city's best selections of pop, rock, jazz, blues and soul. No 7 is devoted exclusively to classical music.
✉ **Carrer Tallers 3 & 7** ☎ **93 318 20 41/93 302 59 46** Ⓜ **Catalunya**

Fernando Selvaggio
Antique books, postcards, stamps, playing-cards, wax seals and a wide range of other memorabilia.
✉ **Carrer Freneria 12** Ⓜ **Jaume I**

Jordi Capell – Cooperative d'Arquitectes
Specialist bookshop for architecture and design, in the basement of the College of Architects.
✉ **Plaça Nova 5** ☎ **93 318 35 51** Ⓜ **Jaume I**

Laie
The best selection of English-language books in Barcelona, including travel maps and guides. There is also a café upstairs.
✉ **Carrer Pau Claris 85** ☎ **93 318 17 39** ⏰ **Café: Mon–Sat 8AM–10PM** Ⓜ **Catalunya**

Musical Emporium
A small shop (despite its grand name) specialising in stringed musical instruments, especially classical guitars.
✉ **La Rambla 129** ☎ **93 317 63 38** Ⓜ **Catalunya**

Norma Comics
Barcelona's largest comic shop sells a huge variety of comics from many different genres.
✉ **Passeig de Sant Joan 9** ☎ **93 245 45 26** Ⓜ **Arc de Triomf**

WHERE TO SHOP

Food & Drink

Brunells Pastisseria
Appears in the *Guinness Book of Records* for making Spain's biggest Easter egg. Try the *torró* (traditional almond fudge), *roques de Montserrat* (meringues) and *carquinyolis* (soft almond biscuits).
✉ Carrer Princesa 22 ☎ 93 319 68 25 🚇 Jaume I

Casa Gispert
Dried fruits, spices, cocoa, coffee, and nuts which are toasted daily in a traditional oak-fired oven.
✉ Carrer Sombrerers 23 ☎ 93 319 75 35 🚇 Jaume I

Colmado Quilez
Barcelona's most famous traditional grocery store, selling an exceptional array of tinned foods, preserves, cold meats and wines.
✉ Rambla de Catalunya 63 ☎ 93 215 23 56 🚇 Passeig de Gràcia

Escribà Patisseries
Many important *Modernista* artists collaborated on the design of this shop. Celebrated for its monumental chocolate cakes.
✉ La Rambla 83 ☎ 93 301 60 27 🚇 Liceu

Formateria Cirera
A little out of the way but worth a visit, this specialist cheese store sells many unusual Spanish cheeses.
✉ Carrer Cera 45 ☎ 93 441 07 59 🚇 Sant Antoni

Forn de Pa Sant Jordi
The long queue outside this bakery is testimony to its excellence. Be sure to taste their *tortellet de cabell d'angel*, a crumbly tart filled with 'angel's hair' (spun candied fruit).
✉ Carrer Llibreteria 8 ☎ 93 310 40 16 🚇 Jaume I

Jamón Jamón
As the name suggests, this shop sells hams and other cold cuts (▶ panel). There is also a restaurant upstairs.
✉ Carrer Mestre Nicolau 4 ☎ 93 209 41 03 🚌 41

Mel Viadiu
Just about every product in this shop is made with honey from the Caldes de Montbui, near Barcelona.
✉ Carrer Comtal 20 ☎ 93 317 04 23 🚇 Urquinaona

Murrià
This *Modernista* store first opened in 1898, and today sells a wide assortment of cheeses, *charcuterie* and other delicacies.
✉ Carrer Roger de Llúria 85 ☎ 93 215 57 89 🚇 Passeig de Gràcia

Planelles-Donat
Specialists in Spanish nougats, made by artisanal methods. Try the home-made ice-creams, too.
✉ Carrer Portal de l'Àngel ☎ 93 317 29 26 🚇 Catalunya

Vins i Caves La Catedral
Wines from all over Spain, with a particularly strong selection from Catalonia.
✉ Plaça de Ramon Berenguer el Gran 1 ☎ 93 319 07 27 🚇 Jaume I

Xampany
The only shop devoted solely to the sale of *cava* (sparkling wine), with over one hundred different varieties to choose from.
✉ Carrer València 200 ☎ 93 453 93 38 🚇 Passeig de Gràcia

Jamón Jamón
Spain is famous for its hams, its cured and smoked meats and its sausages. The quality of ham varies considerably. Expect to pay up to 14,000 ptas a kilo for the best, traditionally cured *jamón Jabugo*. Look out also for the classic, cheaper haunches of *jamón serrano* and *jamón Iberico*, and be sure to try *salchichón*, piquant *chorizo*, Catalan *botifarra* and spicy Mallorcan *sobresada* sausages.

WHERE TO TAKE THE CHILDREN

Children's Attractions

Parks for Children
Most city parks have attractions for children: Parc de l'Espanya Industrial (➤ 65) has a giant dragon slide and a small boating lake; Parc del Laberint (➤ 66–7) has a topiary maze; Turó Parc holds puppet shows at noon on Sundays; Parc del Castell de l'Oreneta offers miniature train and pony rides on Sunday mornings; Parc de la Ciutadella (➤ 64) contains several play areas, a small boating lake and a zoo.

L'Aquàrium
One of Barcelona's newest attractions, and the largest aquarium in Europe. As well as the aquatic life on display, the highlight for most children is the impressive 80m-long tunnel which runs straight through the middle of the shark tank (➤ 72).
✉ Moll d'Espanya, Port Vell
☎ 93 221 74 74 ⏰ Daily 9:30AM–9PM; 🍴 Good
Ⓜ Barceloneta, Drassenes
💰 Very expensive

Beaches
With so much to see and do in the city, it is easy to forget Barcelona's 4km of clean, sandy beaches with children's playgrounds, palm-lined promenades and shower facilities. There is also very good access for people with disabilities.
✉ Platja de Barceloneta, Nova Icària, Bogatell and La Nova Mar Bella Ⓜ Ciutadella, Selva de Mar

Bus Turístic
A circuit around the city on the Bus Turístic with 18 stops at key points of interest is an inexpensive way of allowing children to see the sights. The ticket also covers the Tramvia Blau vintage tram, the Golondrinas pleasure boats, the Tibidabo funicular and the Montjuïc funicular and cable-cars, and gives discounts at the Zoo, Aquarium, Poble Espanyol and Tibidabo Amusement Park.
✉ Plaça de Catalunya (or any of its 18 stops) ⏰ First bus leaves Plaça de Catalunya at 9AM Ⓜ Catalunya
❓ Tickets available for 1 day or 2 days.

Golondrinas (Pleasure Boats, ➤ 72)
A pleasure boat tour of the old harbour or the Port Olímpic is fun for all the family and provides a breath of fresh sea air.
✉ Moll de les Drassanes
☎ 93 442 31 06
⏰ Harbour trips: summer approximately every 20 minutes daily, 11–9:45; out of season: weekdays until 1PM or 6PM; Sat, Sun, and hols until 5PM, 6:30PM or 8PM. Closed 15 Dec–1 Jan. Port Olímpic trips: 11, 1, 4:30 (and 6:30 in summer). Closed mid-Dec to mid-Mar
Ⓜ Drassenes 💰 Moderate

Illa de Fantasia
Europe's largest water park is just north of Barcelona on the coast near Mataró. There is a daily bus from Estació de Sants and Plaça Universitat (☎ 93 451 27 72 for bus details).
✉ Carrer Vilassar de Dalt
☎ 93 751 45 53 ⏰ Jun–Sep 10–7 💰 Very expensive

IMAX Cinema
Older children will enjoy the nature films on IMAX's giant 3-D screen (➤ 72).
✉ Moll d'Espanya, Port Vell
☎ 93 225 11 11 Ⓜ Barceloneta, Drassenes

Montjuïc Funfair
A thrilling amusement park with exciting, stomach-crunching rides, especially popular with teenagers. Younger children will enjoy the nightly, illuminated, musical fountain displays (➤ 18).
✉ Parc d'Atraccions de Montjuïc, Avinguda Miramar
☎ 93 441 70 24 ⏰ Sat, Sun and hols 11AM–9PM 🚌 61
💰 Expensive

WHERE TO TAKE THE CHILDREN

Museu de la Ciènca
The Museu de la Ciènca (Science Museum) is one of Barcelona's most popular museums, and the most important science museum in Spain. Among the attractions, children can lift a hippopotamus, ride on a human gyroscope, feel an earthquake and watch the world turn. Special one-hour guided sessions are given daily. Phone for details.
✉ **Carrer Teodor Roviralta 55** ☎ **93 212 60 50** ⏰ **Tue–Sun 10AM–8PM. Closed Mon. Planetarium shows: Tue–Fri 1, 6; weekends every 45 mins starting at 11.15** ♿ **Good** 🚇 **Avinguda Tibidabo** 🚌 **17, 22, 58, 60, 73, 85** 💰 **Expensive**

Museu de la Cera
The Waxwork Museum is an ideal destination for a rainy day. Pinocchio, Superman and other heroes are all here and don't miss the horror hall!
✉ **Passeig de la Banca, 7** ☎ **93 317 26 49** ⏰ **Jul–Sep: daily 10–8. Oct–Jun: Mon–Fri 10–1:30, 4–7:30; weekends & hols 10–1:30, 4:30–8** 🚇 **Drassanes, Liceu** 💰 **Moderate**

Museu del Futbol Club Barcelona (➤ 54)
A must for all children who are keen on football at this shrine to the game.
✉ **Nou Camp – Gate 14 Carrer Arístides Maillol** ☎ **93 496 36 00** ⏰ **Mon–Sat 10–6:30; Sun and hols 10–2** 🍴 **Café (£)**

Parc Zoològic
Spain's top zoo boasts over 7,000 animals of 500 different species including its main celebrity, Copito de Nieve (Snowflake), the world's only captive albino gorilla. There is also a zoo for the under-fives, where children can stroke farm animals and pets, and a dolphinarium which stages spectacular shows (⏰ Mon–Fri 11:30, 1:30, 4; Sat, Sun and hols 12, 1:30, 4).
✉ **Parc de la Ciutadella** ☎ **93 221 25 06 (Guided tours** ☎ **93 319 81 56)** ⏰ **Summer: daily 9:30AM–7:30PM; winter: daily 10–5** ♿ **Good** 🚇 **Ciutadella** 💰 **Very expensive**

Poble Espanyol (➤ 22)
Children enjoy this open-air 'museum', especially on festa days.

Port Aventura
Catalonia's answer to Disneyland, and reputedly one of Europe's biggest and best theme parks (➤ panel).
✉ **Port Aventura, near Salou** ☎ **93 977/77 90 90** ⏰ **Mar–Oct 10–8 (until midnight in Jul and Aug)** ♿ **Good** 🚉 **Port Aventura** 💰 **Very expensive**

Tibidabo Amusement Park
The charm of this recently renovated fairground, nicknamed *La Muntanya Màgica* (The Magic Mountain), is its authentic, old-fashioned funfair atmosphere with carousels, bumper cars, a hall of mirrors and a breathtaking open ferris wheel (➤ 72). Getting there, on the ancient Tramvia Blau tramline and then by funicular, is exciting in itself.
✉ **Parc d'Atraccions del Tibidabo, Plaça Tibidabo 3–4** ☎ **93 211 79 42** ⏰ **Tue–Fri 1–7PM; Sat, Sun 11AM–9PM** 🚉 **Funicular del Tibidabo** 💰 **Moderate**

Port Aventura
This spectacular new theme park south of Barcelona on the Costa Daurada promises an entertaining day out for all the family with special shops, restaurants, shows and fairground rides in exotic Mexican, Chinese, Polynesian, Wild Western and Mediterranean settings. Top attractions are the 'typhoon' corkscrew ride and the eight 360° loops of the Dragon Khan, Europe's largest roller-coaster.

WHERE TO BE ENTERTAINED

Bars, Clubs & Live Music

When in Spain ...
Barcelonans are night owls, especially on Thursdays, Fridays and Saturdays. The evening begins around 8:30PM with a *passeig* (promenade), followed by *tapas* in a local bar, then dinner at around 10:30PM. Opera, ballet and concerts usually start at 9PM, and the theatre at 10PM. After midnight, music bars become crowded. Around 3AM, clubs and discos fill up and the famous Barcelonan night movement – *la movida* – sweeps across the city until dawn.

Bikini
One of Barcelona's best night spots, with a popular rock/disco club, a Latin-American salsa room and a classy cocktail lounge.
✉ **Carrer Deu i Mata 105** ☎ **93 322 00 05/93 322 08 05** 🕐 **Cockteleria: Mon–Wed 7PM–4:30AM Thu 7PM–5AM; Fri, Sat 7PM–6AM. Rock and salsa rooms: Mon–Thu 11:30PM–4:30AM; Fri, Sat 10:30PM–6AM** 🚇 **Les Corts**

La Bolsa
An unusual bar which lets you play the market at 'The Stock Exchange', where the drink prices, shown on computer screens, fluctuate according to a drink's popularity that night.
✉ **Carrer Tuset 17** ☎ **93 414 70 63** 🚇 **Gràcia**

Cova del Drac
The city's top jazz venue, featuring international names from the jazz world and local talent.
✉ **Carrer Tuset 30** ☎ **93 200 70 32** 🕐 **Mon, Thu 10PM–4AM; Tue, Wed 6PM–4AM; Fri, Sat 9PM–4AM** 🚇 **Muntaner**

Distrito Marítimo
This outdoor bar overlooking the port is a popular meeting-point for weekend clubbers. Open all year.
✉ **Moll de la Fusta** ☎ **93 221 55 61** 🕐 **Tue–Sat noon–4:30AM; Sun 11PM–4:30AM** 🚇 **Drassanes**

Estadi Olímpic
The city's main venue to catch the stadium-filling, mega-star pop concerts. Tickets are best obtained through record shops.
✉ **Avinguda de l'Estadi** ☎ **93 425 49 49** 🚌 **61**

La Fira
Hugely popular 'bar museum', eccentrically furnished with distorting mirrors and other old fairground equipment.
✉ **Carrer Provença 171** ☎ **93 323 72 71** 🕐 **Tue–Thu 10PM–3AM; Fri, Sat 7PM–4.30AM; Sun 6PM–1AM** 🚇 **Hospital Clinic**

Gran Terrassa d'America
Live salsa orchestra at this summertime open-air club on Montjuïc mountain.
✉ **Avinguda Muntanyans, Montjuïc** ☎ **No phone** 🕐 **Varies. Check local listings** 🚌 **61**

Harlem Jazz Club
This small, atmospheric jazz club has long been a favourite of jazz aficionados.
✉ **Carrer Comtessa de Sobradiel 8** ☎ **93 310 07 55** 🕐 **Tue–Thu 8PM–3:30AM; Fri–Sun 8PM–4:30AM** 🚇 **Jaume I**

Jamboree
A choice nightspot for blues, soul, jazz, funk and occasional hip-hop live bands. Upstairs is Los Tarantos, a laid-back bar with predominantly Spanish music.
✉ **Plaça Reial** ☎ **93 301 75 64** 🕐 **Mon–Thu, Sun 8:30PM–4:30AM; Fri, Sat 8:30PM–5AM** 🚇 **Liceu**

Nick Havanna
One of Barcelona's most talked-about bars, thanks to its sensational design. Go late.
✉ **Carrer Roselló 208** ☎ **93 215 65 91** 🕐 **Daily 11PM–4AM (5AM Fri and Sat)** 🚇 **Diagonal**

On/Off
This psychedelic after-hours club plays a standard club

WHERE TO BE ENTERTAINED

mix for the crowds of all-night party-goers who usually turn up around 4AM!
✉ **Camí de la Fuxarda** ☏ 93 423 96 40 ⏰ Fri, Sat midnight–8:30AM. Also Wed–Sun 5:30PM–8:30AM in Jul–Aug Ⓜ Espanya

Otto Zutz
One of the smartest clubs in town, and a *tour de force* of design, with its clever lighting and metal staircases and galleries. Dress smartly and arrive after midnight.
✉ **Carrer Lincoln 15** ☏ 93 238 07 22 ⏰ Tue–Sat 11PM–6AM Ⓜ Fontana, Passeig de Gràcia

Polyester
Trend-setters and techno lovers pack the cement dance floors of this subterranean venue by 3AM. Without doubt, the hottest club in town.
✉ **Estació de França, Avinguda Marquès de l'Argentera 6** ☏ No phone ⏰ Fri, Sat, nights before public hols 1:30AM–any time Ⓜ Barceloneta

Ticktacktoe
Favourite haunt of fashionable, young media executives and TV celebrities who come here as much for the décor and gimmickry as for the cocktails.
✉ **Carrer Roger de Llúria 40** ☏ 93 318 99 47 ⏰ Mon–Thu 8–midnight, Fri, Sat 8PM–1AM Ⓜ Passeig de Gràcia

Torres de Ávila
Design-bar in the Poble Espanyol. Trance-techno discos are staged here at weekends and, in summer, the rooftop terrace bars are particularly magical.
✉ **Avinguda Marquès de Comillas, Poble Espanyol, Montjuïc** ☏ 93 423 93 09 ⏰ Bars: Thu–Sun, 7PM–12:30AM (also Tue and Wed in July-Aug); disco Fri, Sat 1PM–7AM Ⓜ Espanyol

Tres Torres
Beautiful gardens and an elegant courtyard create a sophisticated background for a moneyed clientele. On Thursday nights there is often live jazz or blues.
✉ **Via Augusta 300** ☏ 93 205 16 08 ⏰ Mon–Sat 5PM–4AM Ⓜ Tres Torres

Up And Down
Barcelona's most exclusive nightclub. 'Up'stairs, an affluent, black-tie, post-opera crowd dance, while 'down'stairs, their well-dressed offspring enjoy contemporary club music.
✉ **Diagonal 179** ☏ 93 280 29 22 ⏰ Disco: Tue–Sat 12AM–5:30 or 6AM Ⓜ Sants Estació ❓ Men must wear a tie

Xampanyería Casablanca
A Catalan champagne bar that serves four kinds of house *cava* by the glass, accompanied by a wide range of tasty *tapas* snacks (▶ panel).
✉ **Carrer Bonavista 6** ☏ 93 237 63 99 ⏰ Thu–Sun 6:45PM–2:30AM; (3AM Fri & Sat) Ⓜ Passeig de Gràcia

Zsa Zsa
A sophisticated crowd frequents this elegant designer bar. Don't miss the house speciality – fresh fruit shakes.
✉ **Carrer Rosello 156** ☏ 93 301 85 66 ⏰ 7PM–3AM (3:30 Fri & Sat) Ⓜ Provença

Barcelona's 'Bubbly'
Over 50 Spanish companies produce champagne. Look out for Gramona, Mestres and Torello labels. Catalan champagne is called *cava*, and champagne bars are known as *xampanyerías*. Most serve a limited selection of house *cavas* by the glass, *brut* or *brut nature* (*brut* is slightly sweeter), accompanied by *tapas*. Xampanyet (✉ Carrer Montcada 22), Xampanyería Casablanca and Xampú Xampany (✉ Gran Via de les Corts Catalanes 702) are among the most popular.

WHERE TO BE ENTERTAINED

Theatre, Cinema, Music & Dance

Listings
For entertainment listings, the best source of local information is the magazine *Guía del Ocio*, which previews *La Semana de Barcelona* (This Week in Barcelona). Available from any news-stand, it gives full details (in Spanish) of film, theatre and musical events, and lists bars, restaurants and nightlife. *Informatíu Musical* and the monthly magazine *Barcelona en Música*, available free from tourist offices and record shops, are useful sources of concert information.

Centre Artesà Tradicionàrius
The Centre for Traditional Arts is devoted to the study, teaching and performance of traditional Catalan music and dance.
✉ **Travessera de Sant Antoni 6–8** ☎ **93 218 44 85**
🚇 **Fontana**

Centre Cultural De La Fundació 'La Caixa'
Classical concerts in the splendid *Modernista* setting of Casa Macaya, designed by Puig i Cadalfach in 1901.
✉ **Passeig de Sant Joan 108**
☎ **93 458 89 07** 🚇 **Verdaguer**

El Molino
An old-fashioned music-hall with the traditional variety acts.
✉ **Carrer Vila i Vilá 99** ☎ **93 441 63 83** 🚇 **Paral.lel**

Filmoteca de la Generalitat De Catalunya
Barcelona's official film theatre shows three films a day, usually in VO (original version) with a children's programme at 5PM on Sundays.
✉ **Cinema Aquitania, Avinguda de Sarrià 31–33**
☎ **93 410 75 90**
🕐 **Performance: 5, 7:30 and 10PM. Closed hols and Aug**
🚇 **Hospital Clinic**

Fundació Joan Miró
The Foundation is Spain's main centre for the development of contemporary music and stages a series of concerts (*Nit de Música*) during the summer.
✉ **Plaça Neptú, Parc de Montjuïc** ☎ **93 329 19 08**
🕐 **June–September** 🚌 **61**

Gran Teatre del Liceu
Gutted by fire in 1994 this world-famous opera house is due to reopen in 2001.
✉ **La Rambla dels Caputxins**
🚇 **Liceu**

IMAX Cinema
(▶ 110)

Mercat de les Flors
Innovative dance, drama and music productions.
✉ **Carrer Lleida 59** ☎ **93 426 18 75** 🚇 **Espanya**

Palau de la Música Catalán
Barcelona's main venue for classical music (▶ 59).
✉ **Carrer Sant Francesc de Paula 2** ☎ **93 268 10 00**
🕐 **Box office: Mon–Fri 10–9; Sat 3–9**

La Paloma
Foxtrots, tangos and boleros are still *de rigueur* at the city's famous dance hall.
✉ **Carrer Tigre 27** ☎ **93 301 68 97** 🕐 **Matinees from 6–9:30PM; night dances from 11:30PM–5AM** 🚇 **Universitat**

El Tablao de Carmen
Highly rated flamenco cabaret at the Poble Espanyol. Book in advance.
✉ **Carrer Ares 9, Poble Espanyol, Montjuïc** ☎ **93 325 68 95** 🕐 **Tue–Sun 8PM–1AM (2–3AM at weekends)**
❓ **Shows daily at 9:30. Also Tue–Thu, Sun at 11:30, Fri and Sat at midnight**

Teatre Nacional de Catalunya
Stages performances under the guidance of Josep Maria Flotats. Next door, an auditorium holds symphonic and chamber concerts.
✉ **Plaça de les Glòries**
🚇 **Glòries**

WHERE TO BE ENTERTAINED

Sport

Spectator Sports

American Football
Estadi Olímpic
The 'Barcelona Dragons' play against other teams in the World League on Sundays, April–June. Buy tickets on the day at the stadium.
✉ Avinguda de l'Estadi ☎ 93 425 49 49 🚌 61

Basketball
Joventut
Joventut play league games on Sunday evenings, and European and Spanish Cup matches midweek, September–May. Book tickets in advance.
✉ Avinguda Alfons XIII-Carrer Ponent 143–161, Badalona ☎ 93 460 20 40 Ⓜ Gorg

Bullfighting
Plaça De Toros Monumental
The Bullring and its museum (▶ 56) are open only during the bullfighting season (Apr–Sep). Reserve tickets in advance (☎ 93 453 38 21).
✉ Grand Via de les Corts Catalanes 749 ☎ 93 245 58 04 Ⓜ Monumental

Football
Nou Camp – FC Barcelona
No visit to Barcelona is complete without a visit to Nou Camp, Europe's largest stadium (seating 120,000), and its museum (▶ 54).
✉ Avinguda Aristides Maillol. Museum: Gate 14 ☎ 93 496 36 00 Ⓜ Collblanc, Maria Cristina

Ice Hockey
FC Barcelona Pista de Gel
Barcelona's only professional ice-hockey team. On non-match days, the rink is open to the public.
✉ Avinguda Aristides Maillol 12–18 ☎ 93 496 36 00 Ⓜ Maria Cristina, Collblanc

Participatory Sports

Cycling
Un Cotxe Menys
Escorted daytime and evening cycle tours around the city.
✉ Carrer Esparteria 3 ☎ 93 268 21 05 Ⓜ Jaume 1

Golf
El Prat Golf Club
Just 15km outside Barcelona. You will need to present a membership card of a nationally federated club before you can play here. Phone or write in advance.
✉ Apartado de Correus 10, 08820 El Prat de Llobregat ☎ 93 379 02 78

Horse riding
Hípica Severino de Sant Cugat
Riding lessons for all ages, and treks through the countryside around Sant Cugat and the Sierra de Collserola.
✉ Carrer Princep, Sant Cugat del Vallès ☎ 93 674 11 40

Sailing
Centre Municipal de Vela
Short weekend courses in sailing and windsurfing.
✉ Port Olímpic 100 ☎ 93 221 14 99 Ⓜ Ciutadella

Tennis
Vall Parc Club
Fourteen open-air tennis courts on Tibidabo. Racquets (not balls) for hire.
✉ Carretera de l'Arrabassada 97 ☎ 93 212 67 89 🚌 A6

Tickets
Purchase tickets from the relevant box office or from several ticket offices and booths (*taquillas*) throughout the city. The Centre d'Informació (✉ Palau de la Virreina, Rambla Sant Josep 99 ☎ 93 301 77 75 Ⓒ Mon–Fri 11–2, 5–8, Sat and Aug 10–2) sells tickets for all Ajuntament-sponsored performances. The booth on the corner of Carrer Aribau and Gran Via (Ⓒ Mon-Sat 10:30–1:30, 4–7:30) sells tickets for major pop concerts and most theatre productions.

WHERE TO BE ENTERTAINED

What's On When

Giants & Big Heads
Dancing giants, dragons, *capgrossos* (big heads) and demons play an important part in traditional Catalan folklore. They feature in many *festes*, especially *La Mercè*, with its eccentric *Ball de Gegants*, a dance of costumed 5m-high giants and grinning papier-mâché 'big heads' which is performed from Drassanes to Ciutadella, and the *Corre Foc* (Fire-Running), when devils and dragons scatter firecrackers in the Ciutat Vella.

January
Reis Mags (5–6 Jan): the Three Kings arrive by boat, then tour the city, showering the crowds with sweets.

February
Santa Eulàlia (12–19 Feb): a series of musical events in honour of one of the city's patron saints.
Carnestoltes: one week of pre-Lenten carnival celebrations and costumed processions come to an end on Ash Wednesday with the symbolic burial of a sardine.

March
Sant Medir de Gràcia (3 Mar): procession of traditionally dressed horsemen from Gràcia who ride over Collserola to the Hermitage of Sant Medir (Saint of Broad Beans) for a bean-feast.

March/April
Setmana Santa: religious services and celebrations for Easter Week include a solemn procession from the church of Sant Augustì on Good Friday. Easter celebrations are particularly important in the areas of the city settled by Spaniards from Andalucia and southern Spain.

April
Sant Jordi (23 Apr): the Catalan alternative to St Valentine's Day (▶ 108, panel).

May
Festa de la Bicicleta (one Sun in May): join the Mayor and 15,000 others on a cycle-ride around the city, in an effort to encourage fewer cars.

June
Midsummer (23–4 June) is a good excuse for huge-scale partying and spectacular fireworks.
Trobada Castellera (mid-June): displays of human-tower building
International Film Festival (last two weeks)
Flamenco Festival (last two weeks)
Festival del Grec: arts festival (end Jun–Aug)

July
Aplec de la Sardana, Olot; the biggest *Sardana* dancing festival in Catalonia.

August
Festa Major de Gràcia (15–21 Aug): a popular festival of music, dancing and street celebrations in the Gràcia district (▶ 44–5).

September
Diada de Catalunya (11 Sep): Catalonia's National Day does not mark a victory, but the taking of the city by Felipe V in 1714.
La Mercè (17–24 Sep): boisterous parades and spectacles featuring giants, devils, dragons, big heads and musically choreographed fireworks (▶ panel).
Festa Major de la Barceloneta (end Sep–early Oct): one of the liveliest district *festes*, with processions and dancing on the beach every night.

October
International Jazz Festival

December
Christmas festivities include a craft fair outside the cathedral (6–23 Dec) and a crib in Plaça Sant Jaume.

Practical Matters

Before you go	118
When you are there	119–23
Language	124

Above: *a busy bus stop in Plaça de Catalunya*
Below: *the* Bus Turístic *connects the major attractions*

TIME DIFFERENCES

GMT
12 noon

➔ **Barcelona**
1PM

➔ **Germany**
1PM

⬅ **USA (NY)**
7AM

➔ **Netherlands**
1PM

➔ **Spain**
1PM

BEFORE YOU GO

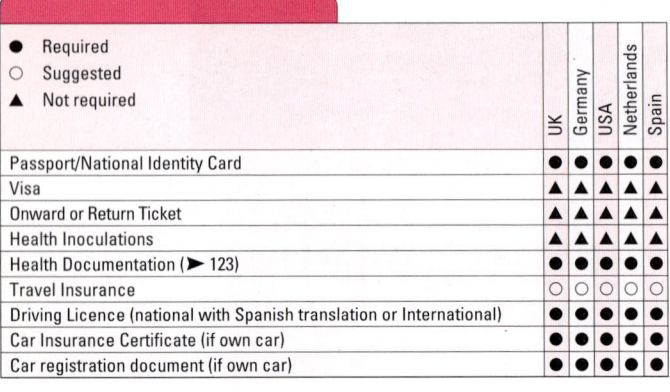

	UK	Germany	USA	Netherlands	Spain
● Required					
○ Suggested					
▲ Not required					
Passport/National Identity Card	●	●	●	●	●
Visa	▲	▲	▲	▲	▲
Onward or Return Ticket	▲	▲	▲	▲	▲
Health Inoculations	▲	▲	▲	▲	▲
Health Documentation (➤ 123)	●	●	●	●	●
Travel Insurance	○	○	○	○	○
Driving Licence (national with Spanish translation or International)	●	●	●	●	●
Car Insurance Certificate (if own car)	●	●	●	●	●
Car registration document (if own car)	●	●	●	●	●

WHEN TO GO

Barcelona

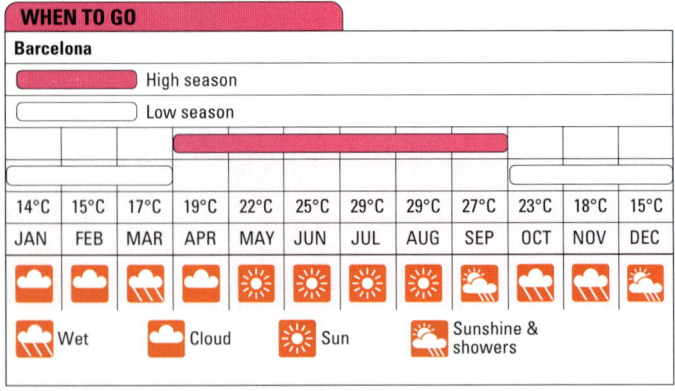

High season
Low season

14°C	15°C	17°C	19°C	22°C	25°C	29°C	29°C	27°C	23°C	18°C	15°C
JAN	FEB	MAR	APR	MAY	JUN	JUL	AUG	SEP	OCT	NOV	DEC

Wet Cloud Sun Sunshine & showers

TOURIST OFFICES

In the UK
Spanish Tourist Office
22–23 Manchester Square
London W1M 5AP
☎ (0171) 486 8077
Fax: (0171) 486 8034
Brochureline:
(0891) 669920

In the USA
Tourist Office of Spain
665 Fifth Avenue (35th floor)
New York
NY 10103
☎ (212) 265-8822
Fax: (212) 265-8864

Tourist Office of Spain
8383 Wilshire Boulevard
Suite 960
Beverley Hills
CA 90211
☎ (213) 658-7192
Fax: (213) 658-1061

CITY POLICE (POLICÍA MUNICIPAL) 092

NATIONAL POLICE (POLICÍA NACIONAL) 091

FIRE (BOMBEROS) 080

AMBULANCE (AMBULÀNCIA) 061

WHEN YOU ARE THERE

ARRIVING

Spain's national airline, Iberia, has scheduled flights to Barcelona's El Prat de Llobregat Airport from major Spanish and European cities. The city is served by 32 international airlines including BA, Delta, KLM, Lufthansa and Virgin Express, and has direct flights to more than 80 international destinations.

El Prat de Llobregat Airport	Journey times
Kilometres to city centre	
	20 minutes
12 kilometres	40 minutes
	30 minutes

Estacio de França Railway Station	Journey times
Near Barceloneta	
	available
Near centre	available
	available

MONEY

Spain's currency is the peseta, issued in notes of 1,000, 2,000, 5,000 and 10,000 pesetas and coins of 5, 10, 25, 50, 100, 200 and 500 pesetas. A one-peseta coin still exists but most bills are rounded down to the nearest 5 pesetas. Travellers' cheques are widely accepted in lieu of cash. On 1 January 1999 the euro became the official currency of Spain and the peseta became a denomination of the euro. Peseta notes and coins continue to be legal tender during a transitional period. Euro bank notes and coins are likely to be introduced by 1 January 2002.

TIME

 Like the rest of Spain, Catalonia is one hour ahead of Greenwich Mean Time (GMT+1), except from late March to late October, when summer time (GMT+2) operates.

CUSTOMS

 YES

Goods obtained duty-free inside the EU or bought outside the EU:
Alcohol (over 20% vol): 1L of spirits *or* 2 litres of fortified/sparkling wine or liqueurs *plus* 2 litres of table wine.
Tobacco: 200 cigarettes *or* 50 cigars *or* 250g of tobacco.
Perfume: 50g
Toilet water: 250ml
Goods obtained inside the EU with duty and tax paid (guidance levels only):
Alcohol (over 20% vol): 10L of spirits *and* 20L of fortified wine or liqueurs *and* 90L of wine *and* 110L of beer.
Cigarettes: 800 cigarettes *and* 200 cigars *and* 1kg of tobacco.
Other goods: No limit
You must be over 17 to benefit from the alcohol and tobacco allowances.

 NO

Drugs, firearms, ammunition, offensive weapons, obscene material, unlicensed animals.

EMBASSIES AND CONSULATES

UK
93 419 90 44

Germany
93 292 100 0

USA
93 280 22 27

Netherlands
93 410 62 10

France
93 317 81 50

WHEN YOU ARE THERE

Turisme de Barcelona
- Carrer Tarragona 149–57
  08015 Barcelona
  ☎ 93 423 18 00
  Fax: 93 423 26 49

Turisme de Catalunya
- Passeig de Gràcia 105–3a
  08008 Barcelona
  ☎ 93 484 98 88

Local Tourist Offices (Oficines d'Informació Turística)
- Barcelona Airport
  International arrivals hall
  (Arribadas Internacionals)
  ☎ 93 478 47 04

- National and EC arrivals
  hall (Arribadas Nacionals
  CEE)
  ☎ 93 478 05 65

- City Centre (Centre Ciutat)
  Plaça de Catalunya 17
  ☎ 93 304 31 35

- Palau Robert
  Passeig de Gràcia 107
  ☎ 93 238 40 00

- La Rambla
  La Rambla 99
  ☎ 93 301 77 75

- Sants Railway Station
  (Estació de Sants)
  Calvià 07181
  ☎ 93 491 44 31

In summer, information booths can be found at Sagrada Família and La Rambla. In the Barri Gòtic, you may also come across uniformed tourist officials, known as 'Red Jackets'.

NATIONAL HOLIDAYS

J	F	M	A	M	J	J	A	S	O	N	D
2		1(1)	(1)	(1)1	(1)1		1	2	1	1	4

1 Jan	New Year's Day
6 Jan	Three Kings
19 Mar	Sant Josep
Mar/Apr	Good Friday, Easter Monday
1 May	Labour Day
May/Jun	Whit Monday
24 Jun	St John
15 Aug	Assumption
11 Sep	Catalan National Day
24 Sep	Our Lady of Mercy
12 Oct	Hispanitat
1 Nov	All Saints' Day
6 Dec	Constitution Day
8 Dec	Feast of the Immaculate Conception
25 Dec	Christmas
26 Dec	Sant Esteve

OPENING HOURS

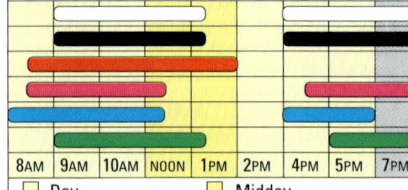

Large department stores and supermarkets may open outside these times, especially in summer. Business hours also vary depending on the season, with many companies working *horas intensivas* in summer, from 8–3. Banks generally close on Saturdays, although some main branches open in the morning 8:30–2. Outside banking hours, money-exchange facilities are available at the airport and Sants railway station. Some *barris* (districts) also have their own separate feast days, when some shops and offices may close.

DRIVE ON THE RIGHT

 **TOILETS FREE**

PUBLIC TRANSPORT

 Metro The metro is the easiest and fastest way of moving around the city. There are two different underground train systems, the Metro (☎ 010) with its five lines identified by number and colour, and the FCG (☎ 93 205 15 15) with two lines in Barcelona and four more lines going to nearby towns.

 Buses Barcelona has an excellent bus network; pick up a free plan from any tourist office. Timetables are also shown at individual bus stops. Buses run 6:30AM–10PM. At night there is a *Nitbus* with routes centred on Plaça de Catalunya. Throughout the year the *Bus Turístic*, a hop-on-hop-off service, circuits the main city sights.

 Trains The Spanish railway system, RENFE, runs trains from Barcelona to all the major cities in Spain and some outside. Many main-line trains stop at the underground stations at Passeig de Gràcia and Plaça de Catalunya. There are two main railway stations: Estació de Sants and Estació de França near Barceloneta.

 Boat Trips The best way to admire the port and coastline is from the sea. Golondrinas offer frequent 35-minute harbour tours or 2-hour voyages to the Port Olímpic (➤ 33). Although Barcelona is the biggest port in the Mediterranean, the only regular passenger services are to the Balearic islands.

 Cable-cars, Funiculars and the Tramvia Blau The Transbordador Aeri cable-car links Barceloneta and Montjuïc and offers fine views. A cable-car connects Montjuïc castle and Intes with the funicular railway. To reach Tibidabo, take the Tramvia Blau, then the Funicular del Tibidabo to the Amusement Park at the top of the hill.

CAR RENTAL

 The leading international car rental companies have offices at Barcelona airport and you can book a car in advance (essential in peak periods) either direct or through a travel agent. Local companies offer competitive rates and will usually deliver a car to the airport.

TAXIS

 Pick up a black and yellow taxi at a taxi rank or hail one if it's displaying a green light and the sign *Lliure/Libre* (free). Fares are not unduly expensive but extra fees are charged for airport trips and for baggage. Prices are shown on a sticker inside.

DRIVING

 Speed limit on motorways (*autopistas*): **120kph**

 Speed limit on main roads : **100kph** On minor roads: **90kph**

 Speed limit in towns (*Poblaciones*): **50kph**

 Seat belts must be worn in front seats at all times and in rear seats where fitted.

 Blood alcohol limit: 8 milligrams per millilitre.

 Fuel (*gasolina*) is available as: *Super Plus* (98 octane), *Super* (96 octane), unleaded or *sin plomo* (90 octane) and *gasoleo* or *gasoil* (diesel). Petrol stations are normally open 6AM–10PM, and closed Sundays, though larger ones are open 24 hours. Most take credit cards.

 If you break down driving your own car and are a member of an AIT-affiliated motoring club, you can call the Real Automóvil Club de España (☎ 91 593 33 33). If the car is hired, follow the instructions given in the documentation; most of the international rental firms provide a rescue service.

PERSONAL SAFETY

The Policía Municipal (navy-blue uniforms) keep law and order in the city. For a police station ask for *la comisaría*.

To help prevent crime:

- Do not carry more cash than you need
- Beware of pickpockets in markets, tourist sights or crowded places
- Avoid walking alone in dark alleys at night, especially in the Barri Xines.
- Leave valuables and important documents in the hotel or apartment safe.

City Police assistance:
☎ **092** from any call box

TELEPHONES

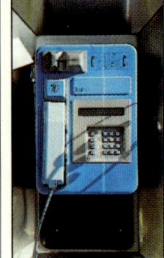

A public telephone (*teléfono*) takes 25, 100 and 500 peseta coins (both new and old). A phonecard (*credifone*) is available from post offices and tobacconists (*estancs*) for 1,000 or 2,000 pesetas.

International Dialling Codes	
From Spain to:	
UK:	00 44
Germany:	00 49
USA & Canada:	00 1
Netherlands:	00 31
France:	00 33

Reduced prices apply to calls made between 10PM and 8AM and on Saturdays after 2PM

POST

Most post offices (*correos*) open Mon–Fri, 9–2 but some also open in the afternoon and on Saturday morning. The main post office (*Oficina Central*) at Via Laietana 1 is open Mon–Sat 8:30AM–10PM, Sun 10–noon, and the Eixample Post Office at Carrer Aragó 282 is open Mon–Fri 8AM–9PM and Sat 9–2. You can also buy stamps at any tobacconist (*estanc*).

ELECTRICITY

The power supply is usually 220 volts but a few old buildings are still wired for 125 volts. Sockets accept two-round-pin-style plugs, so an adaptor is needed for most non-Continental appliances and a transformer for appliances operating on 11–120 volts.

TIPS/GRATUITIES

Yes ✓ No ✗		
Restaurants (if service not inc.)	✓	10%
Cafés/Bars (if service not inc.)	✓	change
Tour Guides	✓	100 ptas
Hairdressers	✓	change
Taxis	✓	10%
Chambermaids/Porters	✓	100 ptas
Theatre/cinemas usherettes	✓	change
Cloakroom attendants	✓	change
Toilets	✗	

What to photograph: *Modernista* buildings, colourful markets, busy street scenes, the Ramblas, the waterfront and sweeping city views from Montjuïc and Tibidabo.
When to photograph: the Spanish summer sun can be powerful at the height of the day, making photos taken at this time appear 'flat'; it is best to photograph in the early morning or late evening.
Where to buy film: film and camera batteries are readily available from specialist shops and *droguerías*.

HEALTH

Insurance
Nationals of EU and certain other countries can get medical treatment in Spain with the relevant documentation (Form E111 for Britons), although private medical insurance is still advised and is essential for all other visitors.

Dental Services
Dental treatment is not usually available free of charge as all dentists practise privately. A list of *dentistas* can be found in the yellow pages of the telephone directory. Dental treatment should be covered by private medical insurance.

Sun Advice
The sunniest (and hottest) months are July and August, with an average of 11 hours sun a day and daytime temperatures of 29°C. Particularly during these months you should avoid the midday sun and use a strong sunblock.

Drugs
Prescription and non-prescription drugs and medicines are available from pharmacies (*farmàcias*), distinguished by a large green cross. They are able to dispense many drugs that would be available only on prescription in other countries.

Safe Water
Tap water is generally safe though it can be heavily chlorinated. Mineral water is cheap to buy and is sold as *con gaz* (carbonated) and *sin gaz* (still). Drink plenty of water during hot weather.

CONCESSIONS

Students Holders of an International Student Identity Card (ISIC) may be able to obtain some concessions on travel, entrance fees etc. Most museums offer 50 per cent discount to students, and many are free on the first Sunday of each month. There are several IYHF youth hostels in the city, with accommodation in multi-bed dormitories. Expect to pay around 1,000–1,500ptas per person.

Senior Citizens Barcelona is a popular destination for older travellers, especially during winter. Most museums and galleries offer a 50 per cent discount for retired people.

CLOTHING SIZES

Spain	UK	Europe	USA		
46	36	46	36		Suits
48	38	48	38		
50	40	50	40		
52	42	52	42		
54	44	54	44		
56	46	56	46		
41	7	41	8		Shoes
42	7.5	42	8.5		
43	8.5	43	9.5		
44	9.5	44	10.5		
45	10.5	45	11.5		
46	11	46	12		
37	14.5	37	14.5		Shirts
38	15	38	15		
39/40	15.5	39/40	15.5		
41	16	41	16		
42	16.5	42	16.5		
43	17	43	17		
36	8	34	6		Dresses
38	10	36	8		
40	12	38	10		
42	14	40	12		
44	16	42	14		
46	18	44	16		
38	4.5	38	6		Shoes
38	5	38	6.5		
39	5.5	39	7		
39	6	39	7.5		
40	6.5	40	8		
41	7	41	8.5		

WHEN DEPARTING

- Remember to contact the airport on the day before leaving to ensure the flight details are unchanged.
- Spanish customs officials are usually polite and normally willing to negotiate.

LANGUAGE

In Barcelona, there are two official languages, Catalan and Spanish, both coming from Latin but both sounding quite different. Everybody can speak Spanish, although Catalan is most commonly spoken. At most tourist attractions you will always find someone who speaks English, and many restaurants have polyglot menus. However, it is advisable to try to learn at least some Catalan, since English is not as widely spoken as in other European countries. Here is a basic vocabulary to help you with the most essential words and expressions.

English	Catalan	English	Catalan
hotel	*hotel*	chambermaid	*cambrera*
bed and breakfast	*llit i berenar*	bath	*bany*
single room	*habitació senzilla*	shower	*dutxa*
double room	*habitació doble*	washbasin	*lavabo*
one person	*una persona*	toilet	*toaleta*
one night	*una nit*	balcony	*balcó*
reservation	*reservas*	key	*clau*
room service	*servei d'habitació*	lift	*ascensor*
bank	*banc*	exchange rate	*tant per cent*
exchange office	*oficina de canvi*	commission	*comissió*
post office	*correos*	cashier	*caixer*
coin	*moneda*	change	*camvi*
banknote	*bitllet de banc*	foreign currency	*moneda estrangera*
traveller's cheque	*xec de viatage*	open	*obert*
credit card	*carta de crèdit*	closed	*tancat*
café	*cafè*	starter	*primer plat*
pub/bar	*celler*	main course	*segón plat*
breakfast	*berenar*	dessert	*postres*
lunch	*dinar*	bill	*cuenta*
dinner	*sopar*	beer	*cervesa*
table	*mesa*	wine	*vi*
waiter	*cambrer*	water	*aigua*
waitress	*cambrera*	coffee	*café*
aeroplane	*avió*	single ticket	*senzill-a*
airport	*aeroport*	return ticket	*anar i tornar*
train	*tren*	non-smoking	*no fumar*
bus	*autobús*	car	*cotxe*
station	*estació*	petrol	*gasolina*
boat	*vaixell*	bus stop	*la parada*
port	*port*	how do I get to…?	*per anar a…?*
ticket	*bitllet*		
yes	*si*	tomorrow	*demà*
no	*no*	excuse me	*perdoni*
please	*per favor*	you're welcome	*de res*
thank you	*gràcies*	how are you?	*com va?*
hello	*hola*	do you speak English?	*parla anglès?*
goodbye	*adéu*	I don't understand	*no ho enten*
good morning	*bon dia*	how much?	*quant es?*
good afternoon	*bona tarda*	where is…?	*on és…?*
goodnight	*bona nit*		
today	*avui*		

INDEX

accommodation 101–3
airport 119
Alt Penedès 13, 84–5
Altafulla 87
Amfiteatre Roma 88
L'Anella Olímpica 32
antiques 108
L'Aquarium 72, 110
Arab Bathhouse 82
Arc de Triomf 64
arts, crafts, gifts and designer goods 106–7

banks 120
Banys Arabs 82
Barcelona Football Club Museum 55, 111
Barcelona Museum of Contemporary Art 50
La Barceloneta 6, 33
Barri Gòtic 9, 38, 40
Barri Xinès 6, 51
bars 97–100, 112–13
beaches 110
bicycle tours 75
boat trips 72, 75, 110, 121
book and music shops 108
bullfighting 115
Bullfighting Museum 56
Bus Turístic 75, 110
buses 121

cable cars 71, 75, 121
cafés 97–100
Canon's House 40
car rental 121
Casa Amatller 36
Casa Batlló 36
Casa del Cánonges 40
Casa de la Ciutat 69
Casa Lleó-Morera 37
Casa Milà 37
Casa Planells 43
Casa Terrades 43
Casa Vicens 45
Catalunya (Catalonia) 7, 12–3, 78–90
La Càtedra Gaudí 60
Catedral, Barcelona 16
Catedral, Girona 82
Catedral, Tarragona 89
Cau Ferrat 86
champagne bars 113
children's attractions 110–11
China Town 6, 51
Church of Montserrat 60
cinema 114
City History Museum 56
Ciutadella Park 64, 110
Ciutat Vella 31, 38–9
climate 7, 118, 123
clothing sizes 123
clubs and live music 112–13
coffee 97
Collecció Thyssen-Bornemisza 49

Coma-Ruga 87
concerts 59, 114
concessions 123
Costa Brava 12
Costa Daurada 12, 87
Creixell 87
crime and personal safety 122
customs regulations 119

Dalí, Salvador 80–1
dental services 123
departure information 124
Drassanes Reials 41
drinking water 123
drives
  Alt Penedès 84
  Costa Daurada 87
driving 118, 121
drugs and medicines 123

eating out 92–100
Ebro Delta 12
economy 7
L'Eixample 9, 31, 42–3
electricity 122
embassies and consulates 120
emergency telephone numbers 119
entertainment 112–16
entertainment listings 114

fashion shopping 104–5
FC Barcelona 54
festivals and events 116
Figueres 801
flamenco 114
Font Monumental 64
food and drink 52–3, 74–5, 109
  see also eating out
football 54, 55, 115
Fundació Antoni Tàpies 44
Fundació Joan Miró 17, 114
funiculars 121

Gaudí, Antoni 9, 14, 21, 24, 37, 45, 57, 60, 64, 69
geography 7
Girona 82
golondrinas 72, 75, 110
Gothic Quarter 9, 38, 40
Gràcia 6, 44–5
Great Royal Palace 68

health 118, 123
history of Barcelona 10–11
Horta 61
Hospital de la Santa Creu i Sant Pau 45

Illa de Fantasia 110
IMAX Cinema 72, 110
insurance 118, 123

King's Square 68
language 124
leisure facilities 7
local knowledge 74–5

Magic Fountain 18
Manzana de la Discòrdia 37
maps
  Barcelona 28–9
  Barcelona environs 46–7
  Catalonia 80–1
  central Barcelona 62–3
  metro 76–7
  Montjuïc and L'Anella Olímpica 34–5
Maritime Museum 41
markets 49, 75
Mercat de la Boqueria 9, 49, 75
La Mercè 39
metro 76, 121
Miró, Joan 17, 66
Miró Foundation 17, 114
Modernisme 6, 31, 36, 37, 42, 43, 44, 45, 54, 57, 60, 61
Monestir de Pedralbes 48, 49
money 119
Montjuïc 18, 31, 110
Montserrat 83
Monument a Colom 50
Museu Arqueològic, Barcelona 18
Museu Arqueològic, Tarragona 89
Museu d'Art Contemporani de Barcelona (MACBA) 50
Museu d'Art Modern (MNAC) 54
Museu de les Arts Decoratives 61
Museu de la Cera 111
Museu de Ceràmica 61
Museu de la Ciència 111
Museu de l'Empordà 81
Museu Etnològic 18
Museu Frederic Marès 55
Museu del Futbol Club Barcelona 55, 111
Museu de Geologia 64
Museu d'Història Catalunya 58
Museu d'Història de la Ciutat 56
Museu d'Història, Tarragona 89
Museu de Juguets 81
Museu Maricel de Mar 86
Museu Marítim 41
Museu Militar 18
Museu de la Música 43
Museu Nacional d'Art de Catalunya (MNAC) 19
Museu i Necropolia Paleocristians 89
Museu Pau Casals 87
Museu Picasso 20
Museu Romàntic 86
Museu Tauri de la Monumental 56
Museu Tèxtil i d'Indumentària 57
Museu del Vi 85
Museu de Zoologia 64
Museum of Catalan History 58
Museum of Graphic Arts 22
Museum of Modern Art (MNAC) 54

125

INDEX

Museum of Popular Arts, Industries and Traditions 22
museum opening hours 120
museum shops 106
music 59, 114

national holidays 120
National Museum of Catalan Art 19
national parks 13
nightlife 112–13

Old City 31, 38–9
Old Port 6, 72
Olympic Games 32, 73
Olympic Ring 32
opening hours 93, 120
orientation 6

Palace of Catalan Music 59
Palace of the Deputy 68
Palace of the Sea 58
Palau Güell 57
Palau de la Música Catalana 59
Palau de Lloctinent 68
Palau de Mar 58
Palau Quadras 43
Palau Reial Major 68
Palau Reial de Pedralbes 61
Parc del Castell de l'Oreneta 110
Parc de la Ciutadella 64, 110
Parc del Clot 65
Parc de la Creueta del Coll 65
Parc de l'Espanya Industrial 65, 110
Parc Güell 21
Parc de Joan Miró 66
Parc del Laberint 66, 110
Parc Zoològic 111
Passeig Arqueològic, Tarragona 89
passports and visas 118
Pavelló Barcelona 66
Pedralbes district 60
pharmacies 120, 123

photography 123
Picasso, Pablo 14, 20
Picasso Museum 20
Plaça de Catalunya 67
Plaça del Rei 68
Plaça Reial 69
Plaça Sant Jaume 69
Poble Espanyol 22, 107, 111
police 119, 122
population 7
Port Aventura 111
Port Olímpic 33
Port Vell 6, 72
postal services 122
public transport 76–7, 121

La Rambla 9, 23, 31, 51
La Rambla de Canaletes 23, 51
La Ribera 6, 26, 39
Royal Palace of Pedralbes 61
Royal Shipyards 41

La Sagrada Família 245
Sanchez Vicario, Arantxa 14
Sant Martí Sarroca 84
Sant Pere de Riudebitlles 84
Sant Quintí de Mediona 84
Sant Sadurní d'Anoia 85
Sant Salvador 87
Santa Maria del Mar 26
Santes Creus 84
sardana 16, 69
Science Museum 111
senior citizens 123
Serra de Collserola 73
shopping 1049, 120
Sitges 86
Spanish Village 22, 107, 111
sport 115
street sculptures 33, 71, 74
students and young travellers 123
sun protection 123
tapas 74–5, 95

Tàpies Foundation 44
Tarragona 88–90
taxis 121
Teatre-Museu Dalí 80–1
telephones 122
Textile and Clothing Museum 57
theatre 114
Tibidabo 31, 73
Tibidabo Amusement Park 73, 111
time differences 118, 119
tipping 122
toilets 121
Torredembarra 87
tourist offices 118, 120
Town Hall 69
Toy Museum 81
trains 121
Tramvia Blau 75, 121
travelling to Barcelona 119
Turó Parc 110

views of Barcelona 75
Vila Olímpica 73
Vilafranca del Penedès 85
Vilanova i la Geltrú 87

walks
  Barri Gòtic 40
  L'Eixample 43
  Pedralbes district 60
  La Rambla 51
  Tarragona 90
  waterfront 70–1
waterfront 31, 70–1
waterparks and amusement parks 110–11
Waxwork Museum 111
Wilfred 'The Hairy' 14
wines and wineries 53, 85

youth hostels 123

Zona Alta 61

Acknowledgements

The Automobile Association would like to thank the following photographers, libraries, associations and individuals for their assistance in the preparation of this book.

DACS 17; **MARY EVANS PICTURE LIBRARY** 10b; **TERESA FISHER** 21b, 38b, 43b, 54, 57a, 58, 70b, 75a, 84b,122a,b,c; **HULTON GETTY** 14c; **MRI BANKERS' GUIDE TO FOREIGN CURRENCY** 119; **MUSEU PICASSO** 20b, 20c; **NATURE PHOTOGRAPHERS** (R Bush) 13a; **POWERSTOCK** Front cover (c); **REX FEATURES** 14b; **SPECTRUM COLOUR LIBRARY** 9c, 25, 27b, 52b, 53c, 87b; **WORLD PICTURES** 51b

The remaining pictures are from the Association's own library (AA PHOTO LIBRARY) and were taken by STEVE DAY with the exception of the following;-

PHILIP ENTICNAP Front cover(a), 5b, 13b, 19b, 23c, 61, 78, 79, 80a, 81, 82, 83, 84a, 85a, 85b, 88a, 88b, 89a, 89b, 90a, 90b.

PETER WILSON Back cover, 11b, 12b, 17b, 22b, 26b, 26c, 36, 41, 49, 50b, 53b, 55, 59b, 67b, 69b, 73b, 85b, 86.

Copy editor: Susie Whimster   Page layout: Stuart Perry